MW01234774

"Helping others to understand *The Art of Juggling* is both timely and necessary for the world today! This book is a great guide for anyone trying to fit '30 hours of responsibilities into a 24-hour day'. Thank you for sharing!"

Dr. Jan Cardwell, *Vice-President/Director*
University of Phoenix – Detroit

"This book is a masterpiece which is full of effective strategies for better multi-tasking."

Dr Bob Harrison
America's Increase Authority

"In an era where we want to have it all Sylvia Jordan's book *The Art of Juggling* is a necessity! An essential guide for the modern-day woman striving to be "every woman"! Her shared wisdom in helping women recognize their season in life is imperative in helping this generation flourish!"

Acquanita Thorpe, *Stay At Home Mom*
former Bank Assistant Vice President

The Art of
JUGGLING

---*---

The Successful Woman's Guide
to Finding Balance in Life

SYLVIA JORDAN

emerge
publishing
TULSA, OKLAHOMA

22 21 20 19 18 17   8 7 6 5 4 3 2 1

THE ART OF JUGGLING — The Successful Women's Guide to Finding Balance in Life

©2017 Sylvia Jordan

Published by:

TULSA, OKLAHOMA

Emerge Publishing, LLC
9521B Riverside Parkway, Suite 243
Tulsa, Oklahoma 74137
Phone: 888.407.4447
www.EmergePublishing.com

Library of Congress Cataloging-in-Publication Data

ISBN: 978-1-943127-53-5   Paperback
         978-1-943127-54-2   E-book

BISAC Category:
REL012130 RELIGION / Christian Life / Women's Issues
SEL023000 SELF-HELP / Personal Growth / Self-Esteem

Printed in the United States of America.

TABLE OF CONTENTS

DEDICATION

This book is dedicated to the loving memory of my son, Jared Lawrence Jordan.

In our short time on this earth, we don't always have all the answers. In fact, we what we really have are many questions that are often left unanswered. And I will never understand why this special young man was suddenly called to Heaven at such a young age. Maybe I'll never know. But he will always be my baby. And my life has been forever changed by his presence. I am blessed and proud to have been his mother, friend and confidant in his short, but full, life.

Jared, my first born, transitioned from us at the tender age of 31, totally unexpectedly. I was in the process of completing this manuscript when a piece of my heart was suddenly taken away without warning...or reason.

Jared was an amazing young man: fun, caring, loving and giving. And he gave me many a juggling lesson over the years. And on many occasions, he also made the art of juggling that much easier.

Whenever I returned home from food shopping he was the child that always said "Mommy, let me help you carry those

1

groceries in." Talk about making the job easier! He was always a compassionate and extremely giving child. He was overly sensitive as well, causing me to juggle a few extra pins as he was the one who constantly need more hugs, special classes and glasses...and just one more peanut M&M (You'll get to read about that tale later in the book, along with other anecdotes about my loving, but often stubborn, eldest child).

Jared, my son, you will be forever loved and your memory forever cherished. I look forward to the day that I shall get to hold you in my arms once more, in that special place we always talked about- Heaven.

INTRODUCTION

Throughout my life, I've come to realize that the traditional methods of managing tasks are not effective for everyone. It may be a simple task for some mothers to juggle life with a mate, multiple children and a full-time career, while others may find it more challenging particularly a single parent mom. With the many happenings of life, it's understandable why many of us struggle to simply make life work and accomplish our biggest dreams along the way. I've read countless guides that promise to teach you how to get organized, how to make it all work and the funniest of all…how to fit 30 hours into your 24-hour day. These were all great reads and offered some very valid points, however not every detail is designed to improve the way in which YOUR life operates.

I became easily frustrated when I couldn't seem to manage the norms of family, career, school, social circles and achieving my personal goals. I felt less accomplished and believe it or not, sometimes I felt like I was failing at life. Many times, it felt as if I was holding a hand full of pins and they would all begin to stick me in the palms of my hands at once, causing extreme pain. That's it…life became painful in a sense and I'm certain, it wasn't supposed to feel this way. I admit, as women, we sometimes pick up more than we should in life but most of us are conditioned to believe that we can juggle most of what we grab. The scary part is, you can probably juggle much more than you believe you can.

When you look at the professional juggler, they attempt to maneuver or rotate several objects in their hands without dropping them. The professional juggler is skilled in keeping several objects in motion in the air at the same time by alternately tossing and catching them.   I'd like to think of our lives as a juggler and the objects being "pins", like a bowling ball pin. A pin is any responsibility, task, goal, undertaking, duty, mission, assignment, desire, position, or the pursuit of a dream that you are doing that will require you to manage multiple responsibilities at one time.

You must put the pins you grab into perspective and manage them properly. Expect to drop one occasionally, as you will sometimes fail to complete a task but never be afraid to start over. Most importantly, learn how to toss a few pins around and make them all work to your advantage.

Multi-tasking has been my strongest attribute and I've always managed to get things done. This was much easier when it was just me and all I really had to manage was morning coffee, what to wear and a work schedule. However, life progressed and my desire to do more increased also. I wanted to give more. I needed to live out my purpose, without compromising family, friends and most importantly, my dreams. The moment I realized that I don't have to do everything at once, was the moment I mastered the art of juggling the pins of life.

I wrote this book because I have been asked the questions over and over again. How do you do so much? How have you manage to hold a political position while married to a pastor of a growing assembly? How did you find time to write your books? How do you go after your dreams while working? How old were you children when you started to do "you"? How does your family handle all you are doing? And trust me the lists of questions have been ever increasing.

I'm here to tell you that it takes first of all fortitude to decide that you first of all want to juggle, what you are going to juggle and deciding how many pins you want to juggle. In this book you will be faced with the decisions, the challenges, joys, fulfillment of juggling with picking up and putting down pins.

There is no "One Size Fits All" in the world of managing tasks or juggling. The ability for one person to maneuver work, social activities, church, classes and family may not be the same for others. If there were one set of rules for getting it right, we would all be on the fast track to success in living. This is what makes it such a challenge because we are not all the same and we don't all want the same things out of life. My dreams may not be yours and your aspirations are not the same as your neighbor or friend. There is one common factor, we all have pins that we choose to juggle and some that we absolutely must juggle. The art of juggling is founded on your strength to choose those pins that are assigned to you and to have the mindset to put down those pins that are not yours to juggle. This book will help you to identify the difference in your pins and those of others. Without this process, you will never accomplish the art of juggling.

Through trial and error, I have discovered that there are many beneficial methods to help with the successful completion of multiple tasks. The rewards of accomplishing your dreams and goals in your life are immeasurable.

As you continue to read, you will notice that there is a common concept: many of the suggestions are created for realistic, outgoing and everyday tasks that many women must face. However, they are systematically designed to be applied to very personal situations that allow you to make them work in your life, according to your goals and the tasks you have at hand.

Instead of trying to take on too many tasks and force yourself to make them work, you learn to choose the ones pins that are most exciting for you and to do so, only when they are in season. In other words, choosing not to pick up a pin right now doesn't imply that you can't or won't have the opportunity to pick it up later. Allow yourself to focus on what makes you happy for a change. You've spent a large part of your life doing what makes others happy but what about your happiness? What about your purpose? You must realize that you have a purpose in life and it's up to you to accept the challenge it brings. Your friends, family and loved ones will be just fine and those that really love you will be proud to see you doing something for yourself for a change.

The pins are plentiful and your strength is amazing but you don't have to juggle them all...only the ones that matter most to you. This is the one thing that has helped me accomplish much of what I have today. I hope it offers you the same or greater results as you juggle from day to day.

It is my sincerest hope that I have offered you a source of genuine hope regarding the pins you want to pick-up, as well as the mindset to drop a few of those that you don't really need right now. Your results can be amazing but the sense of self-assurance you gain will be phenomenal, once you discover that you are more than enough and have what it takes to succeed in all that you set out to accomplish.

Much of my inspiration to never give up on my dreams has come from others. I enjoy seeing others take on the challenges of life and come out on top but eventually, I grew tired of watching and decided to pick up my own pins and accomplish more than I ever thought possible and I want to encourage you to do the same.

Chapter 1

The Whys of Juggling

The existence of woman is an art in itself and for many, existing is only the beginning of greatness. At this very moment, there are women all around the globe that are focused on their next move, while still completing steps from last week. You guessed it. These are the women who juggle the everyday challenges of life and then some. They thrive on getting "ish" done and welcome the challenge that says they will never be able to do everything they have on their plate. Not only will they fill their plates, they will serve it up in healthy portions because the juggling woman never gets enough.

The key to being the woman who juggles without dropping the pin is that she has made the decision to make an impact with her life while maintaining balance in her life. In her mind, nothing is impossible and doubt has no place in her life. When doubt is removed, fear is evicted and all else becomes absolutely possible. This is not the attitude that every woman takes on in life and in fact, juggling the ins and outs of life, is not for the faint of heart. Is it for you? You must be the deciding factor in that equation because juggling is a decision that only the strongest woman can make and successfully achieve. Not only can it be done, many women around you are doing it. Your neighbor, coworker, boss or even the barista that serves your morning coffee may be mastering the art of juggling.

My Story

Everyone hits that time and place in their lives when they realize that they want to do more and achieve more with their lives. You want to be more, experience more...not just simply exist and watch life pass you by. You may feel that at this juncture in your life you finally have all of your balls in the air, so to speak, or all of your ducks are in a row and you are ready to take on a bold and daring new facet of your life, to enter a new dimension.

Well, for me, this happened at that time of my life where I had been a "stay-at-home-mom" of two wonderful, energetic school-aged children. I felt like my life was going according to plan (better than I had planned actually), but I felt as though I needed to do something for myself. I knew right then and there that it was time for me to pick up a new pin and juggle things up a bit. I knew deep down that I had so much more to give than simply being a full-time, loving wife and mother. I wanted to leave my mark on the world and give back to my tiny, close-knit community. It was time to make a difference in my personal life, as well as the world around me.

Don't get me wrong, I am fully aware of the joys of motherhoods. Raising my two children was extremely rewarding and fulfilling, but it was just one dimension of my life and I was extremely grateful to be blessed with such an amazing, loving family. However, there was a deep longing in my heart for "something more" and I realized that this yearning was't going to simply fade away.

After many nights of in-depth discussions with my husband in which we weighed my options, discussed the timing of my realization and the "season" of our lives, and additional guidance from my parents, I realized I was more than ready to pick up another pin and keep juggling. I decided I was going to run for city councilman.

My parents, though always supportive, were a bit old-fashioned. They believed a woman's place was in the home... period....end of story! My dad had always been the sole breadwinner of our family, which consisted of him, my mother and nine children. My mother never worked outside of the home while any of her children were still living under her roof. It wasn't until her early 50's that she finally decided that it was time to enter the workforce. She took a job at a local private preschool as a teacher's assistant. With nine of us, she certainly had plenty of experience in child behavior!

I recall a discussion I had a one point and time with my mother where I let her know what a huge impact she had on my life. My mother had many balls in the air in her life as a wife and mother: raising nine children, taking on custody of a twelve year old niece, a grandchild, cleaning, cooking and baking, gardening, laundry for a house full of people, caring for both her husband and an aging mother, and being a doting grandparent. She was also actively involved in the church and was a friend to many as she was a great listener. During our chat, I let her know that she was my role model for a well-rounded woman, a true inspiration. She was everything I wanted to be...and more! She herself had the need to do more with her life at the young age of 50 when she decided to become a full-fledged working woman. I can honestly say, she fully understood where I was coming from, as an expert life juggler herself.

As women, we all have that pivotal time in our lives where we realize we want to do more. We feel as though we have that inner voice that wants to be heard. However, we must also realize that we must continue to expertly juggle the already existing pins in our lives. It's crucial to maintain a healthy balance. Only you can know when it's time to throw in that extra pin and juggle on!

The Juggler in You

You will be amazed at the ones who have more going on than you would ever imagine. The woman who seems to have it all together and never stressed about anything going wrong in life, is usually a professional juggler. No. She didn't attend any classes or take tests to master the art of juggling things in life, but she has and still does burn the midnight oil. Juggling requires sacrifice and dedication that often sees no end or light in the tunnel. The outcome is always positive because in managing several things, several people are often helped along the way. Juggling is a step above multi-tasking and will require a person to always be at their best. There are many important factors to consider when maneuvering several tasks in life and the most important is good health. There is an ongoing list of things to be done but in order to be effective in juggling these things, you must feel great. An adequate supply of rest, exercise and good nutrition are the primary ingredients to feeling your best. One must realize that in doing multiple things in life, an abundance of energy is required. Introduce healthy vitamins into your lifestyle and don't cheat on sleep. It is easy to become fatigued from doing so much, but if you are well rested and properly nourished, you can approach every obstacle and task with full potential.

Women are designed to demand and dominate in many areas of life. Take for instance the innate ability a woman has to nurture, display a creative spirit, embrace special talents, love, motivate, (give hugs when needed) and so much more. These are all leading characteristics required to juggle many of the tasks and challenges that life presents. As a woman you know your worth but do you realize your value? There are things that women were designed to do that man could never fathom and this alone makes you a unique species. If you have the God given ability to carry a child inside your body and nourish it to development for delivery, you are aligned to juggle! You have taken the first step by making the decision to do so and that is the biggest step you will have to take. Now, it is time to take each task with stride and do it in your very own way, without fear, without doubt but with determination and a big applause because you are absolutely AWESOME!

There is no clear description of what should or should not be juggled but with your approach and determination, you are the perfect description of who should be juggling. Do you believe this? It is imperative that you have faith in everything you set out to do before you do it. Faith is an important element in life, and must be an anchor in life while juggling. Plan accordingly and say out loud that failure is not an option. It is not a psyche but a statement of determination that only you can bring to life. Stop feeling like you can't accomplish something simply because it has never been done before. You could very well be the first! Make an effort to stand out more and you will see the difference between juggling and managing. Strive to accomplish some of the things you have been putting off for years. Now is the perfect time because tomorrow may be too late.

The list of women that started something when no one believed in it but them, the list is long and getting longer by the day. Many times people shine negative light on the goals of others because they have yet to accomplish anything. Remove these people from the equation of your life because there is nothing good to come from negative energy. Surround yourself with positive people who will exert positive influence on your juggling habits because this is where you will receive the gist of your "Get Up and Go" mentality. Do not be afraid to connect with others you have noticed juggling things and doing it well. You can learn a lot from a juggler, especially an experienced one. Ask questions and inquire about their routines and what makes it easier for them to manage several things at once. This is not to say you will copy their initiative but intertwine it with your own strategy to make it work for you. I believe ever juggler needs a mentor. Someone who you see is juggling quite well. Watch and learn from them.

Every juggler has a story of how things seemed to be too much at first but the ability and the determination to overcome those obstacles is what allows them to succeed in the art of juggling. You can take the negative insight given and use it as the source to fuel your fire to get up and going. Above all else, be smart about it. There is no way that you will juggle multiple things in life and not have issues or obstacles arise. The key is to not give up but instead, remain steadfast and deal with every obstacle head-on. Remember, Rome wasn't built in a day and your juggling acts won't all come together at once either. Expect setbacks, problems, discouragement, difficulties, frustrations and disappointments. Then take a second to realize that all of these things are a part of life, and although you are not immune to them, you don't have to fall victim to them either because you are a juggler. When you fall down, or many of your pins fall, the key to remember is to GET BACK UP!

Take a self-examination of yourself and get in sync with those things you want to do right now. Research, plan and execute to get things going and before you know it, you will be doing the very thing that they said you couldn't or wouldn't do. Take a moment, a day or a week to decide on some of the things you want to add to your list of things to juggle. Make it count and don't scratch it out once it is added because of fear that it is too much to handle. This is the time that you have allocated to own every aspect of your life and do what makes you feel complete and happy. Juggling is not a chore but a chance to live life out loud and enjoy every moment of it.

The foundation for your success as a juggler is blended with three ingredients, convenience, necessity and obligation. Women must approach each new assignment with these ingredients on board. Not every pin you pick up is your own to carry. Often times you will be asked to do things that will in no way contribute to your cause or benefit your purpose. These are the pins that will stick you in the hand and cause you to drop other things that are important or beneficial to you.

It may be convenient for others to ask you to do something but is it equally as convenient for you? Is it a necessary part of your purpose or do you simply feel obligated to do what has been asked of you? If you have to second-guess yourself with a certain pin, walk away from it. In fact, run away from it and leave it for someone else to deal with because it's not your problem and definitely not your pin to juggle. The things you choose to juggle should give you a feeling of accomplishment but also present a challenge.

Your planning process will involve the basic essentials you will incorporate to make these things happen as often as they are required. Your research has helped you to develop a clear plan on how to execute every task you approach. This is the research, plan and execution strategy that will get you through each day, one task at a time. There is no right or wrong way to do it, but there is the way that works best for you and nothing else matters in the art of juggling.

Now that you know exactly what you want to do, what will it take to get you up and moving? First of all, you've taken the first step by making the decision but let's get you in action. Your life's mission statement has been clearly identified by the person that matters most, you. Before a bodybuilder enters a competition, she focuses on the areas that need attention and dedicates the time and energy to perfecting those areas to ensure a possible win. You may not be preparing for a bodybuilding competition but the art of juggling is equally as strenuous on the body. Therefore, you must now focus on your weaknesses and work to strengthen those areas.

Do you procrastinate often? Do you find yourself giving up easily? Are you horrible at time management or perhaps always tardy? These are the types of questions women ask themselves as they prepare to condition their physical and mental self for juggling. Be honest with yourself and you will not go wrong but come out stronger than ever in the long run. Start to look at life as a journey that you've already missed half of and now you are eager to catch up. This means that there is no time to wait but you must change those bad habits, strengthen those weak areas and stand boldly and confident as you juggle one pin at a time.

Prepare to be judged and not on your juggling skills. This new mindset that you will adapt as a juggler will change the way people view you and that is to be expected. Not only is it to be expected but it is absolutely okay. You have nothing to do with what people think about the way you do things, as long as you are accomplishing the goals you set out to achieve. Do not give in to the snarls and frowns you are guaranteed to receive because your hands are filled with things that are important to you. People will never clearly understand why one does what makes them happy when it means not doing for others every time it is asked. Just as you have the right to do for others, you have the same right to do for yourself. You will become enthusiastic at the idea of getting things done that you have put off for so very long. Your life will take on an entirely new meaning and the feeling of accomplishment you have is unexplainable. Eventually, people will see you as you see others who juggle. They will wonder how you manage to get it right, over and over again. It will puzzle them that you are indeed doing so many things and making a difference not only to others, but to yourself as well. These are the very thoughts you had of others not so long ago and now, you are that juggling sensation.

Not Your Ordinary Woman

Juggling is not for the ordinary woman but for the one who hungers to live a life of success in her career, relationships, self-fulfillment and community worth. There is no space for comfort in the life of a juggler because it is a constant cycle of clutter that you commit to juggle effectively. The funny thing is, it becomes a burning desire to juggle and without it, a woman begins to feel null and void. This is a reminder that not only does juggling tasks in life benefit others but it delivers a sense of completion to the woman doing so. Challenges arise daily and this is one sure sign that you are doing something right. You have surely seen jugglers in the act of juggling items such as balls or other objects. Notice the look on their face as they balance and juggle each item. Stern attention and a notable presence of anxiety can be seen as well. It is no different for a woman juggling work, family, community programs, after-school activities with the kids, non-profits, church activities, writing that first book and the list goes on and on. You are pushed outside of your comfort zone and sometimes you will feel the urge to jump but your determination to not drop one single pin keeps you in sync with everything you have going on in life.

Most women have a juggling foundation but the decision to erect a structured way of life from this foundation is one that only the bold and daring woman will make. Orbiting around this foundation is easy to do but designing a blueprint, picking up the tools and building a life complete with juggling is a choice that is made when the woman wants to experience an elevated sense of happiness. The thrill and high is like no other and once you begin the process, quitting is not an option. As a juggling woman, you are in control of your own happiness, but most importantly, you are in control of your success in life. Changing your attitude towards the tasks you take on can greatly change the outcome of whatever you set out to do. There is more than one way to experience great rewards as a woman who successfully manages many tasks or overcomes various obstacles. It begins with the decision to do so and is successfully carried out with a surmountable amount of effort. There is a great deal of happiness to be gained when a great deal of effort is put forth towards anything a woman sets out to do in life.

Mental clarity is important when balancing several acts and for women, focusing is the lead character. It is crucial that one who has committed to the art of juggling is mentally focused and committed to making it their primary goal. It is essential that every opportunity to balance be seized in order to achieve the ultimate success, which results in utter happiness. You will be required to completely reprogram your body and your thought process in order to learn how to associate happiness with your accomplishments. It is almost like you are returning to school and class is in session. The difference is that you are the pupil and the instructor and each test will be more difficult as time progresses. Sounds stressful? Great! You have the right idea and understand exactly what to expect. The reprogramming process involves a total reset and complete overhaul of your self-management, career-related and interpersonal skills. It is almost as if you are creating an entirely new you. Don't allow this to alarm you because if you think about it, the original you couldn't possibly handle what you are about to take on. Prepare to be the best you possible and set your eyes and thoughts on accomplishing what you never imagined. This is the mindset of not just any juggler but a successful juggler like you.

As a juggler, you immediately transform from an ordinary woman to superwoman. Yes, you have super powers and you are going to use each and every one of them. In fact, you will often use these powers without even noticing they have been activated. Women fail to realize the hidden power that exists within everyday experiences and challenges that surround them. The objective is to counter these experiences and take control of them mentally in order to physically manage them as they occur. One of the hidden gems in the life of a woman who juggles successful is mindfulness. You must be mindful of your surroundings and things that happen in your life. It keeps you on top of situations and in control of those events or challenges as they occur. Here is a secret weapon of most successful women who are managing multiple things in life, meditation. It may sound over the top or perhaps time consuming if you really have your hands full but it is necessary and can help you overcome many obstacles before they occur. This is a happiness booster that delivers the mental clarity needed to accept what comes and rise to each occasion.

You are now the woman who has so much going on that there doesn't seem to be enough hours in the day, but that is okay because you are no ordinary woman. The way you view your life is a large part of the way you approach each pin you've picked up. Take a positive approach and never take your eyes off of the end result, which is to juggle effectively. Mornings will turn to nights that turn to days that turn to weeks and for you, this is life as you will learn to love it. Your dedication to making things work and servicing those areas in life that are most important to you will be the fuel that ignites the energy for every pin you balance. The spark will always be aflame and your primary obstacle is to put out every blaze without getting burned. You have your hands full and you wouldn't have it any other way because this is life and it excites you!

The Happy Juggler

Nothing confuses a negative process more than happiness and a smiling face. This is the confidence that you wear daily knowing that you can handle the most difficult of challenges. The meditation, preparation and anxiety all blend perfectly to result in happiness with a great big smile. This is why many people will think that something is surely wrong with you because they see you doing it all and doing it well. But what they can't figure out is how you manage to do so many things and seem to never be stressed but always smiling. Only a woman that juggles could truly understand your journey and the joy you've found along the way. This is in no way to imply that you will be happy in everything you do but instead, you will see the good in all you do. In each pin you pick up, the good should definitely outweigh the bad and it is this that causes you to smile and feel completely happy about your juggling process. That's the one thing that makes juggling an art. You don't look for happiness in what you do, it simply finds you in the yielded results. Imagine the number of people that run around day after day attempting to get one thing done. At the end of the day, the task is unaccomplished, they're completely worn out and a sensed of failure consumes them. Your approach to all things complicated is designed to prepare for success before you begin the process and this is what makes you unique.

Juggler's work in a rhythm during their balancing acts and you must adopt this ritual in order to successfully juggle every pin. Shift your focus on the end result and imagine the sense of reward that exists within that climax. It is truly a matter of the heart and as a juggler, you begin to take care of your very own heart. It is almost as if you exhale with the juggle of each pin. Every woman enjoys the relief of a nice big breath and each time you accomplish a task, it's as if you've taken a breath of fresh air. The truth is that with your initial mound of success in juggling, you will experience an immeasurable amount of joy. This is the feeling that you will begin to crave and in order to satisfy your craving, you know exactly what it takes and you don't mind doing it. It becomes addictive and you just can't get enough.

The happy juggler is one that does it naturally, as it has become a normal part of life for her. She expects challenges, obstacles and even failures but they never get the best of her. In fact, they revamp her energy and align her for greatness in her next attempt. In the act of balancing, you will rarely ever be successful in juggling every pin. It kind of defeats the purpose if you know that everything you set out to do will be a success. Each pin you pick up will be a risk because life is filled with them and you are challenging life to the fullest as a juggler. "Whether you think you can, or you think you can't, you're right" – Henry Ford. You must think yourself into happiness and know that you are the key to your success as a juggler. You will find that the more you have to balance, the more you want to take on. It easily becomes a way of life and anything less seems unfulfilling.

At this point, your feelings are likely all over the place. There is probably a little lump in your throat, which is anxiety and you may even have sweaty palms. It's all completely normal for the woman preparing to take on her biggest role in life, being happy in all that she does. You are about to experience life like never before and best of all, you will be in complete control. No pin will fall unless you drop it but get this, it's absolutely okay to drop one every once and a while. Just be certain to pick it up and try again. It is actually the dropped pins that help women to perfect the art of balancing the many things in life that they take on. Your career, family, friends, social commitments and personal goals are all on the same plate but you don't have to pick them up all at once. The key is not to over indulge but to simply indulge in the few things you have taken on as a challenge. Be proud of what you are attempting to do and your willingness to just get it right. Think about the thousands of women out there that wonder how you do it and have no clue that you have simply made the choice to get things done and be happy about it. For the first time in life, you are in control of your very own happiness and all you had to do was pick up the pin, one at a time and get your juggle on. The feeling that you have right now, that knot in your stomach or extreme joy in your heart, it's the feeling that comes with every pin. You never knew anxiety could feel so good but just wait until you start to balance the pins that you've chosen. Forget that, don't wait! It is time to make your debut as the woman who made the choice to juggle and find happiness in doing so. Take a look at the list you made and decide which pins you can't wait to grab hold of and begin to balance. There's no time like the present and them earlier you start, the sooner you finish!

Here are a few points to ponder if you are considering a life of juggling.

- Juggling is not something that yields overnight results
- Balancing goals will take a huge mental commitment
- This is a decision you must make for yourself and no one else
- Juggling is a perfect way to find the happiness in what you desire

CHAPTER 2

THE DEMANDS OF JUGGLING

Dreams vs. Reality

When my husband and I got officially engaged we began to have the typical "serious" discussions about our future together. I'm sure that every newly engaged couple does the same, once the initial "newness" of the proposal wears off, once you come down from Cloud 9 and reality hits. You begin to discuss where you will live, if you will have children and how many, what you need to buy, honeymoon details...and of course, the big event itself...the wedding ceremony! This alone leads to a series of discussions: the venue, guest list, menu, flowers and so forth.

This gives you plenty of time to dream, but it is also essentially a wake-up call. Once the initial bliss of becoming engaged wears off, you are faced with the reality of building a future together, which is an amazing thing, of course. But it also involves a lot of time, planning and creating and balancing (and adhering to) a budget as well. You need to stay grounded and make decisions, which you know you can reasonably accomplish. It's great to dream big, but you also have to be realistic as well. You are planning for a lifetime together and a potential household full of children as well. You know longer have the option of living paycheck to paycheck. You need to be able to cover your daily living expenses, monthly bills and save for the future as well. This is a pivotal time in a relationship, as some couples often have differences in these areas.

Surprisingly, as do most young lovebirds, my new fiancé and I agreed on almost everything. We had both been brought up in the traditional two-parent household. However, his mom worked outside of the home during his childhood while mine didn't reenter the workforce until she had raised the lot of us.

We come to the conclusion that I would resign from my full-time job and raise our children, when the time came along. Our plan of action was to wait about 5 years before we even thought about starting a family of our own. We wanted to have some time together, just the two of us, to celebrate our union and enjoy each other's company, as well as ensure that we were financially stable before bringing children into the scheme.

Raising children entails a great deal of financial responsibility: medical bills, diapers and all of the other various sundry items that come along with a newborn, not to mention food, clothing, furniture, education and so forth. Yes, it is more than worth it, but one should always make sure they are financially able to handle the additional expenses before making the decision to bring children into the household.

Of course all of this sounds great when you are thriving on the windfall of two steady incomes, as well as living in the moment, without any real financial burdens to worry about. We were enjoying our day-to-day lives as a newly married couple, basking in our love and savoring every moment so you can imagine our surprise when I discovered that I was pregnant just a year into our newlywed bliss! I was going to be giving birth to a baby boy!! This of course, was not part of our "5 Year Plan" so of course we had to reassess.

While I was overjoyed at the imminent arrival of our son, I had fully come to terms with the fact that I would soon be a full-time stay-at-home mom. I was looking forward to raising my beautiful bundle of joy. However, I was not ready to be stuck in a financial rut. I dreaded having to deal with the inevitable calls from bill collectors and I felt extremely guilty for no longer being able to contribute to our current financial situation.

With medical bills, the cost of raising a newborn, saving for the future and so on, as well as our regular bills, we knew that it was going to be a struggle. This of course, led to the necessary demand for me to pick up another pin and start juggling. I made the decision to ultimately return to the workforce. I was lucky to have the ability to return to a job that not only was a steady source of income, but one that I loved and that brought joy to my life. Of course, this made juggling the pins in my life just a tad easier.

By now you have figured out that juggling is demanding. In fact, just the mere thought of all of the things you have on your plate is overwhelming. It's okay because you have aligned your mental and physical self to successfully accommodate any overwhelming circumstances that may arise. You have signed on for a role that most people shy away from and it is up to you to meet the demands presented by juggling. These pins that you have picked up are not the only aspects of life you have to approach because there is still a great deal of other things that can't be put aside. No matter which pins you choose to juggle, there are a few that stay in your hands at all times. Family, career, health, shopping, school, etc. These are the things that are here to stay and must be managed along with the other things you have committed to juggle. Prioritizing is an option at this point because you don't want to sacrifice anything of importance in order to juggle those pins you've committed to juggle. Balance is the bridge that you will utilize to successfully reach your destination of completion in juggling and taking care of the other essentials of life.

Scheduling is efficient, necessary, and it is an important part of the process. In order to become effective at scheduling, you must learn to prioritize and organize. Put first things first and organize your method of approach in all of your tasks. There are many tools available for women who are juggling multiple tasks. Research these tools, try them out and find out which of those work best for you to accomplish your goals. Technology has taken a front row seat to almost every game in life and it also has its place in organization. Digital alerts, schedulers and tasks companions are out there to help you get organized and to help you remain accountable. Accountability is a must in every task you attempt to juggle because failure has its consequences and you never want to pick up a pin that you know you will drop later because you weren't prepared. Accountability cannot only be a digital tool, but a faithful, loyal person that can keep you on track. A close friend that will be honest with you and keep you accountable to what you have committed to balance. I really think this accountability is essential in order to be a success juggler.

The Balance Equation

For most women, juggling the demands of a career, family, personal goals and other things is an ongoing challenge. The fact that you have committed to juggle these things and so much more, already distinguishes you from most women but the challenge remains constant. Considering the way things are in this day and age with companies expecting more from employees and coworkers being extra competitive, that alone can be a challenge to juggle. Conquering the perfect balance can easily seem impossible but because you have undergone the necessary mental and physical preparation, the challenge must be prepared for you. The mentality that it is necessary to do more with less these days is what keeps most women out of the circle of success in the balancing acts. The key is to create your own greatness and be the "more" that you lack in every equation. Every pin that you have picked up is yours to juggle but balancing it isn't enough, you've got to balance it effectively and conquer the challenge.

It is necessary for you to take a close look at where you are in life right now and what's important to you. This is the only way you can accommodate the demands that juggling will have on your life. Are your children young and dependent upon you for almost everything they do? Is your spouse or significant other really clingy or always relying on your time? Do you have aging parents you are responsible to care for?

Do you oversee certain clubs or organization where the team members are not dependable, which leads you to handle most of the responsibility? These such questions are the ones you must ask yourself as a juggler because it is at this point that you must develop a tough skin. Your days of niceness and eagerness to please others are no more. It is the first day of the rest of your life as a woman with a plan to prioritize, organize and successfully manage every pin she touches. Your name will be associated with all things great because your ability to accommodate many things will allow you to overcome amazing challenges in life. Juggling is an art but only you can design the final image of the canvas on which you juggle. It's all in the way you balance, the precision with which you build and the eagerness you have as you toss each pin.

One aspect of balancing the equation is clearing out the clutter. This is the fun part. Well, it is fun to watch and will feel great for the woman that tackles this task head-on. As a woman, you must know that life is often times filled with clutter. This is described as anything that occupies space in your mind, heart or life but has no meaning or offers no benefits. In order to juggle, you have got to clear out the clutter! Zone in on those things that are important to you and forget about the extra stuff. Most of the time, the extra belongs to someone else who has chosen to throw it off on you or you've taken it on because you're just that nice. You're still nice but now you're going to practice being nice to yourself for a change. Imagine the joy you would have if you looked out for yourself as much as you looked out for others. As you consider all of the things that you really don't need in your life, take the steps to get rid of them. It doesn't have to be done all at once but don't take too long because the more clutter you have, the less room you will have to juggle. It doesn't mean that you are a rude and uncaring person. Absolutely not. It just means you are beginning to rid your life of some clutter, extra weight, letting go of a pin. Those extra carpools that you're taking just so the other mom can make her exercise class, let them go! Your early arrival to work to help your coworker who never rises to the occasion, stop it! Your volunteering to work every athletic concession for your son's school, stop it! This is the clutter that will keep you from being great at juggling your own chaos.

Build a Wall

This may come as a shock because many women spend a large part of their lives trying to tear down the wall. As a juggler, a wall will be necessary to keep out the unwanted. It is the process of redesigning yourself to connect with only those things you want on your side of the wall. People who show up unannounced or invited won't have access to you anymore. There must be a value placed on your time and your worth, and it is up to you to make certain that you present yourself at face value. Get rid of the guilt that you allow to linger in your life. Now that you are a juggler, you will have the determination to accomplish every task you take on but as mentioned earlier, some pins will fall. Those super powers you have, they don't make you superwoman in the realistic form. You know she's fictitious and couldn't compete with half the things you do. Stop feeling guilty if you miss an occasional picnic or can't make lunch with a friend. It's life. You're busy and the pins are waiting.

Don't become so consumed with the idea of juggling that you fail to let others assist you. It's a natural part of the art and actually the only way to be successful at doing it. Enlist the help of those you feel will benefit your overall objective. In most cases, people are eager to help you accomplish the things you've set out to do and they don't have an ulterior motive in doing so. Your book may be your top priority and you know it will be great but don't hesitate to have a trusted pair of eyes take a look at it. That event you are planning has the potential to be phenomenal but utilizing the services of other professionals can make the process a lot easier. Here's something you probably didn't realize. Picking up the pins doesn't mean you can't allow someone else to hold them for a while, just to create a meaningful balance. You are on track and can expect to achieve much of what you set out to balance because of your willingness to incorporate the essential tools into your juggling act.

Your commitment to balancing multiple things is to be applauded but don't expect everyone to render a round of applause. There are many things in life that women set out to accomplish and other people, especially other women, don't celebrate their accomplishments. Don't expect everyone to rally behind you in what you are doing and because of this, you should know that not everyone will be in your corner. Be selective of who you allow on your side of the wall because there is always a negative Nancy that can't wait to see you drop a pin. These are the ones that have absolutely nothing going for them and thrive from seeing others fail. If you've developed a firm foundation, they will never be afforded the opportunity to see you fail. Be conscious of your circle, your inner circle and it is even best to keep it small. Limit the conversation that involves the many things you have going on. It really isn't necessary to discuss these things with people who aren't helping you in some way. Look at it as extra protection or the security system for the wall you've built.

Balance this if you dare! Place a book on the counter in front of you, leaving it open so you can read it.

Got it? Now, place your right index finger above your right eye and your left pinkie behind your neck.

You doing okay?

Now, move your right index finger in a circular motion just above your eye, and simultaneously use your left pinkie finger to tap the back of your neck.

That's not it, you're not done yet.

Continue to navigate the instructed directions with both fingers while tapping your left heel and saying *supercalifragilisticexpialidocious* (just a word used when there is nothing else to say) three times really fast.

It's difficult to do all of these things at once, right?

You bet it is because juggling anything in life is a challenge and let's not mention that you never even remembered to try to read the book.

Juggling is supposed to be challenging. The acts were originated back in Egyptian times and juggling various areas of life has been around much longer.

It matters not how good you are or become at juggling multiple things. It is always a good idea to take a step back and see how well you are actually juggling your pins. Any feelings of dissatisfaction should be closely examined. Anything you have on your plate that isn't fun or fulfilling anymore should be immediately removed. This is the only time you should trade in a pin. It's not a suggestion to drop it and free up some space, but instead replace it with one that is more rewarding for you. Sometimes, something as simple as restructuring your technique could be all it takes to accomplish the overall goal.

It is true that juggling is a technique but it is also supposed to deliver feelings of accomplishments when done correctly. Your energy rejuvenates from the positive feelings that success in juggling yields. Most importantly, it is meant to make you happy, confident, and to always feel in control of whatever obstacles or tasks you have taken on. This is the backdrop to the pretty picture that is painted which displays the happy woman who is always juggling multiple tasks. The saying goes that things aren't always as they seem and for a juggling woman, things always seem to be just as they are, complicated and necessary but that's exactly how you like it.

Finalize the Formula

Your art of juggling tasks is visually different than the art of an artistic juggler but take a moment to actually watch a great juggler one day. It is obvious that if he or she attempts to juggle too many items at once, he begins to focus solely on one thing or has trouble balancing. The outcome is that he will lose footing or drop the items being juggled, which will throw the entire act off balance. This is exactly what happens to a woman if she attempts to juggle too many things at once. The successful balance of family, church, work, school and social activities requires the exact same approach as artistic juggling. In order to keep everything aligned, you must take the same approach as a professional juggler in order to keep the flow consistent. Limit your activities and commitments, divide your time and focus among the things you have taken on and develop a solid foundation from which you can work.

You are capable of balancing the act as long as you formulate a proper structure from which you balance. "You have within you the strength, the patience, and the passion to reach for the stars and change the world." -Harriet Tubman. This is the mindset that must become the qualifying factor of each pin you approach. It reassures your confidence, validates your worth and submits to your strength. Life can easy lose its footing and throw simple activities out of whack. As a juggler, it is essential that you maintain stability in your tasks, stand boldly and strong as you work towards each goal and always keep your eyes on the end result. It is easy to become distracted by things that are of no benefit to your tasks and this is where the strength in mind and agility becomes more relevant. In the equation of juggling, you must always remain the constant factor that creates the balance for a successful solution.

Limitations in life are necessary, especially for a juggler, but incorporating them isn't always easy. The horizon of things that occur in life changes as often as the time and there is essentially no way to know what will come. The most efficient approach when collecting pins is to select from a healthy group of options. Consider choosing pins from the four basic groups: mental, social, physical and personal. A fulfilled life will involve activities and tasks from all of these groups and as a juggler, you should commit to those that are most valuable to you and your happiness, and purpose in life. Once you've gathered a group of pins, select the ones that you like most. Don't pick up a pin to juggle because you think it will make others proud or be of benefit for them. It is important to remember that this entire process is about your very own happiness, your life purposes, and success in juggling. If you are doing this for recognition or praise, you are doing it for the wrong reason. As a juggler, your objective is to satisfy those areas of your life where you feel less accomplished. Possibly for the first time in your life, it really is all about YOU!

Now that you've identified the equation and developed a formula to complete it, don't complicate things by over exaggerating the method. Simply put, don't pick up more pins than you can juggle at one time. It can be difficult to eliminate pins from your plate because you have a strong desire to get things done. Keep in mind that you will have more than one opportunity to juggle. The process involves picking up a pin as you've completed another or completing an entire cycle of pins before moving on to another group. The beauty of it is that you are in control of how you juggle because it is you that controls the success of the entire cycle. Doesn't that give you a strong sense of reassurance? In your process of juggling you will encounter many things that you wish to pick up and add to your stack. Remember to be patient, the time for that pin will come but not until you've successfully juggled each pin you currently hold.

The common denominator to successfully balancing the equation of juggling is to perform from a solid foundation that is structured on an overall goal. A goal that helps you to recall why you started juggling in the first place. Think about where you are in life and where you long to be. Stand steadfast in your belief and desire as you work to elevate your level of happiness. You know your worth and settling for less is not to be accepted on any level. If you can juggle all of your pins while managing to keeping you balance and staying on track to your goals, you will have an easy time with the journey of juggling the many tasks of life. Determination and dedication will be the caffeine for your daily thoughts. It is always possible to refill your cup, each time you pick a different pin up. Just be sure to drink from the cup as often as needed because you never want to become fatigued when working towards something you really want to achieve.

On those days when you don't feel your best or you feel that you can no longer continue to juggle as much as you have been, take a break from it all. It is your prerogative to rest whenever it is needed. You must know that there is no professional juggler who goes at it nonstop. Rest is essential and a vital part of a healthy life for any juggler. It is this time that you use to revitalize your mental and physical energy. Women find different ways to spend this time off and it all comes down to what works best for you. Retreat to something that you truly enjoy but be sure that it has nothing to do with the pins you are juggling. Take in a concert, enjoy an evening out doing something you love, such as dancing, painting or cruising the time. It is your time to unwind and feel carefree because you have no pins to juggle at all.

You are at a point of total transformation as a juggling woman and there is nothing anyone can do about it. The opportunity to reinvent yourself and everything you stand for knocked and you were brave enough to answer. There are a few things you will have to consistently remind yourself of as you juggle and it is addressed several times here. Remain positive and remove negativity! This is crucial for a healthy juggling journey. This is stressed because one ounce of negativity can drain you and cause you to lose sight of what is really important, the pins you are juggling day by day. It is never okay to allow negative people, things or energy to occupy space in your life. This is a factor of disaster in any equation and the balance is almost always impacted. You, like many others have a happy place and the best way to identify the negativity is to analyze it and determine if it fits in your happy place. If it seems out of order or causes you to experience any level of discomfort, throw it out!

There are several methods to be taken when attempting to remove any negativity from your path in life. Here's something you should remember. Negativity is never invited into your life but will almost always crash your happiness party. Just when you think you have a good grip on all of your pins and everything is moving along just fine, in comes the negative and your entire balancing act could lose its potential for greatness. Do not sabotage your own journey by attempting to entertain the negative energy brought on by someone or something else. The impact this can have on your health, life and entire journey could potentially lead to complete demise of everything you have worked so diligently to establish. Doing so will cause you to juggle your emotions instead of your pins. You will be up one day, filled with joy and down the next, crying because it seems everything is crashing down around you. Don't allow the fear of success to frighten you out of your calm approach to the balancing act you have going on. The very moment that a woman feels things are going too good, she will begin to look for the bad. Guess what? It is completely possible that you are just that good! Celebrate it and don't deny yourself the right to feel fulfilled in all you do. Essentially, as you juggle multiple things there will be an occasional drop of the pin, but that is only a reminder that you are human and capable of starting over.

You are probably wondering how to identify those things that are negative and mean more harm than good. In addition to being able to sense that something just isn't right, there are a few other indicators. Negativity exists in different forms and though it can't be physically touched, you will feel the difference in it and positive power. Conversations that make you want to run for the hills and never look back is a sure sign of negativity. People that make critical comments about what you are doing and how you are doing it are definitely negative forces that need to be removed. Be sure to avoid anyone that is constantly complaining about their circumstance or position in life but do nothing to change it. You are on a mission to be successful and feel accomplished for doing so, negativity will reroute your mission and cause you to crash and burn.

Once you have identified the negativity, get rid of girl! Become aware of what's going on around you. As a juggler, this will become a natural instinct but you must take control of what goes on in your space. Don't be victimized by the negative energy but channel your strengths and evict it. Another thing you must do is stop wasting time trying to convince negative people that what you are doing is a good thing. This is a waste of time because the negative people in your life have one agenda, to ruin whatever you set out to accomplish it. Know that they are going to stick to their plan to do so and it is up to you to shut them down. Create a space for those things that are important to you and secure them with your passion for success. In other words, allow nothing negative to invade your happy space by only allowing those people that are supportive of what you are doing into your space. These are the people that you could possibly even trust your pins with when necessary.

During your reinvention process, become resilient. Create calm and relaxing atmospheres that help you to maintain your inner positive peace. Your reinvention will actually include a detox because you are ridding your body of the entire negative and filling it with things that make you smile and feel good about life. You will know that your detox is working because you will begin to see things much clearer and even your pins will seem to be smaller than they are. Organization comes naturally for you and the amount of peace you have reflects the level of happiness you display. One of the biggest rewards from creating a balance is that you will become a beacon of light for others around you. Although you are not doing this for praise or recognition, it makes you feel good to know that others think what you are doing is simply amazing. You made the decision to embark upon a journey of juggling, analyzed the demands and took the necessary steps to overcome the obstacles that accompany those demands. You my lady, are on your way to being an efficient juggler with ambitious potential!

Here are a few points to ponder to help you meet the demands of juggling.

- You must manage your time wisely
- Giving up is not an option
- Don't allow interference from others to distract you from your pins
- Get rid of all negative influences that are in your life

CHAPTER 3

WHAT'S YOUR SEASON OF LIFE?

Seasons come and seasons go and we expect it because that's just how life is. The saying is that everything has its season but what about every person. Is there a season for them? The answer to this is a simple but firm, yes. Seasons don't just happen in the climate but they also occur in the lives of women every day. As babies, it's our season to blossom into cute little girls that are curious to learn as much as we can about everything around us. It is in other seasons that women are in school to learn and decide which path they will take in life and let's not forget the season to find love and live life to its fullest. So yes, seasons come and go for as long as we live but it seems that there is a certain season in everyone's life in which they find their inner self. It is the season that defines the greatness of a woman and gives her the breath of fresh air that she has longed for in life. What is your season in life? This is a question you must ask, especially once you have made the decision to become a juggler. Women need to know their season in order to help them live life to the fullest and it also helps them to approach the pins they juggle on a daily basis. Your season gives perspective on where you are in life and why you approach things in the manner that you do. It helps you to better understand the feelings you have and your response to those feelings. Every area of life has its season. For instance, as a student there is a season of studying, applying what you have learned in an intern, graduation and moving on to a career. It all seems to happen so fast but that is exactly how seasons evolve, at an extremely fast pace.

I was very fortunate to have been blessed with an amazing mother, a wonderful woman who embraced her life and lived it to the fullest. She loved deeply: her husband, her children and just about anyone she met. And she was loved deeply by many as well. However, my amazing mother, having raised 9 children, been an adoring wife, while running a household and later returning to work, was now entering a new season in her life. She was starting to become forgetful. It was little things at first: where had she placed her keys? Why did she come into the kitchen at 10:00 at night? What was the date of the church bake sale? I was so busy trying to juggle all of the pins in my life that I was not as attuned to these early signs of dementia as I should've been. Looking back now, these little subtleties were early warning signs that my mother was starting to exhibit the early stages of dementia.

I was the responsible daughter...the one who took my mom to her countless doctor appointments: primary care physician, podiatrist, and so forth. I also took her to run errands as well:

the bank, the pharmacy, grocery shopping and the like. My siblings had mentioned that I should ask her doctor about her now frequent forgetfulness, as it was starting to become a daily event and our once "on the ball" mother was starting to forget to turn off the oven or forgetting names of loved ones. We were all becoming a more than a bit concerned about her mental health. She has always been our rock, the one who reminded us to send out birthday cards and not to forget our sweater when it was cold. It pained us deeply to see her start to decline.

So of course, at her next doctor's appointment I mentioned this to her primary care physician and you can imagine how crushed I felt when he asked her "Who was just elected President of the United States?" and my mother's stunned reply was "I really don't know.....Hmmmm, I can't remember." I felt my heart drop.

Barack Obama had recently been elected and my family had always been deeply involved in politics so my mom not knowing the name of the new President Elect was like a man not knowing the name of the quarterback of his favorite football team!

At this moment, I knew I was about to enter a new season of my life, and my mother's as well. Her soon to be diagnosed dementia was going to affect every member of our family. We would now have to become the joint caregivers of the woman who had raised us and taught us everything we knew about how to behave, how to parent, how to love. The roles were suddenly reversed. She became the child and we were to become the parents.

Obviously, this was hard on my mother as well, as she was always strong and independent. To have to surrender that part of herself was a huge challenge. She was going from a season of being the loving nurturer and provider to being the one that needed nurturing. You can imagine how hard this adjustment must have been for her.

This new season affected all of us deeply: of course my mom, my siblings and myself, as well as our spouses and children. The entire family had to ban together to form a plan on how to provide for our mother, who had always been a pillar in both our family and the community. She was loved and respected by everyone with whom she had ever spoken and it pained us to see her slowly decline.

We knew that with this season would come many changes, many shifts in responsibility and family duties, changes in family get-togethers, not to mention the pain of watching the stronger person you know start to change before your very eyes. We had to deal with our pain while remaining strong for our mother. We had to become a united force as we entered this new season of our lives as adults. Every single one of us had to pick up an extra pin or two and keep juggling.

You must embrace your season with everything you have in order to capitalize on its full potential. Just as a gardener has a timetable for planting and harvesting, as a juggler you must do the same. Gain a clear understanding of the best time to take on certain projects. Research to ensure that it is a good time to pick up a pin or if perhaps it is best to wait on that particular one. There is really no need to take on the task of preparing your plants for indoors when it's the season for them to be outside. It doesn't make much sense and is a complete waste of time. In other words, pick up your pins according to your season. If it's a season in your life when work is demanding and you have several deadlines to meet, don't take on the PTA president and Girl Scout leader positions because a pin will drop and something will suffer. If you are diligent in your commitments and really know your season, you will embrace it and take it as an opportunity to do things that will turn out great because the atmosphere and circumstances around you are aligned for success.

Knowing your season permits you to know what to expect. There are times when juggling that you will find it necessary and even okay to walk away from certain leadership positions. You may have been an overachiever and joined just one too many social clubs. In due season, you may have that chance but not until that season arrives. Let go of some of the extra and set realistic expectations as you juggle. You will not get everything right in life but when you make space for those things that are truly important, you are setting the margin for success. The desire to juggle everything at once may be strong but the need to do so is simply not there. You have time and the more balanced your pins are, the better the outcome. You seek to yield positive results and picking pins during their season helps to ensure a healthy harvest. Once you have a clear picture of the season you are in, you can prepare to approach tasks with a clear mindset because the current climate of your life is perfect for a sunny outcome.

Perseverance is a major factor in knowing your season in life. This is true because your present season is not necessarily your permanent one. There are many occasions when you are required to persevere and push through much of the unwanted in order to arrive at the desired or a more comfortable season. It's almost like the weather in some ways. We endure a bit of harsh cold during the winter because it is expected that warmer days are ahead. We completely understand that the beautiful days filled with sunshine will come, but only in their season.

The same mindset is required for juggling and its alike in many ways. You push through the most challenging moments and even pick up a few sharp pins occasionally, but the fact that there is a greater reward in the end causes you to persevere and not give up. You can't forget about hope because it is your saving grace in many tasks. Those days when juggling seems to be more than you can imagine and you grow tired of what you've taken on, it is then that you rely on the hope that you're doing something that will one day be rewarding to you. Seasons exists in life because as humans, we need change, consistent change. It isn't to say we don't need the sunshine, the cold or the rain but we don't need those things all the time. The hope that sunshine will rise after the cloud is always a substantial motivator for women who juggle the most challenging things in life.

In all that you do, know what season you are in during each phase of your life. It's all about timing. Let me share a story with you.

I served as a city councilwoman in my city for seventeen years. I met some incredible people during those years. I witness the start and development of some awesome businesses. The journey was more than I could ever imagine.

After wrapping up my political career, and putting this pin down, I was given an offer that I simply could not refuse. It would however require that I pick up another pin. I was offered a wonderful opportunity to be a board member with a company/ community organization that was doing outstanding work on the local and global spectrum.

I met privately with the president of the organization and he confirmed that I had been vetted ad would be a key component on the board of directors. They had not been able to find someone like myself to fill the position. Now, I must admit, he was saying everything I wanted to hear. In addition, I fully agreed with the board's vision and mission, but knew deep in my heart, it was not the right time for me to join the board.

I was extended an invitation to attend the next board meeting. Following the board meeting, which was three hours long might I add, I knew it was not the right time. My decision was not based on the length of the meeting, which usually are relatively short from what I'm told. But from the expectations that were clearly laid out in regards of what I was expected to do. Again, timing was just not right and I did not want to disappoint those expecting a certain level of performance from me.

A key component of taking on a pin is that you are planning to juggle. You do not take on a pin, knowing in your mind that you are going to drop it.

Your name is on the line.

This is one of my long-term goals, but the timing wasn't in sync with my life. Following the board meeting, I knew it was going to be crucial for me to meet with the president of the company and share with him my concerns.

After speaking with him, he clearly understood and extended a position of consultant to the president. In essence, he asked if I could be his personal consultant. I would not be required to attend the board meetings, but he would keep me abreast of all pertinent information. Win-Win! All because I carefully observed and managed my pins.

Push Through to Your Purpose

There will be times in life when you feel that you are going crazy and chances are, you aren't far from it but you must remember, as a juggler, you're not an average person and a little bit of crazy lives in us all. Your decision to become a juggler was likely motivated in part due to a lingering question you asked yourself, "What is my purpose?" This is a very common question and one that often leaves many women perplexed and at a loss but as a juggler, it is easy to determine your purpose, once you recognize your season. The desire to know and understand your purpose is life will exist in us all because we were created with a purpose. The decision to juggle is aligned with that purpose because your objective is to feel significant in your lifetime and have a positive impact. Unfortunately, there are many things, events and trials that exist in life that will cause us to lose sight of our purpose and sometimes that makes it hard to fulfill it. Your purpose will be your passion and it provides the foundation you need to perservere and rise to the demands of juggling.

It's easy to become so consumed and lost in your search that you lose sight of what's really important. You no longer realize the strength and power you possess as a juggler. The power to work through to reach your purpose and genuinely define what it is and why it was assigned to you. This is all a part of your journey as a juggler, because knowing your season helps you to nourish your purpose, which in turn will provide a successful balance of the pins you pick up. That being said, you should know that your purpose is subject to change at any time. This isn't to say that you'll never be completely on track with what your purpose really is but it is proof that some people have more than one purpose in life. This is especially true of women who make the decision to juggle. Each day you live your life as a wife, mother, boss, employee, mentor, mentee, etc. but the doing so simply becomes a part of your purpose in life. You may have found that being a wife or mother is one of the most rewarding parts of your life but it doesn't mean that you give up on your dream or desire to be the best business owner because you're dedicated to being a good mother. You create a balance that allows you accept the demands that juggling brings and you push through to get things done.

How many times have you found yourself in a friendly competition of some kind with friends, coworkers or others? More than likely, quite often. Although you knew it was all in good fun, the desire to win or come out on top was likely burning deep within you. This is the exact same feeling you experience with the demands of juggling. The difference is that you are your own competition and you never want to let yourself down. You push through to do better each time, you focus a little more this time and perhaps start a bit sooner to finish stronger. All of these are a part of the process of finding your purpose during your season. You take notes as you go along and find out which environments are best for your performances. You surround yourself with fans that will cheer you on and push you to greatness. This is no longer just a balancing act but it is a journey in life that you have chosen and believe it or not, you've fallen in love with. Your vision is clear and the objective now is to stay the course and realize the importance of your purpose.

Just as your roles change in everyday life, they will also change as you juggle pins from day to day. This is why it is important to realize that it is normal to have more than one purpose in life and not spend too much time searching for that one purpose. Your purpose can widely be determined by your season. It is vital that you recognize your season and your purpose and once they are recognized, embrace them both. Women miss out on so much in life because they spend years searching for that one thing they are destined to do, when it is clearly visible that a woman of your strength has more than one assignment while here on earth. Opportunities are missed, pins are dropped and expectations are shattered because the purpose driven search is not as most would have it to be. A good rule of thumb is that if you are doing something that truly makes you happy, gives you fulfillment, makes a difference in the world and isn't always easy to do, then you are more than likely working towards your purpose.

Women spend a lot of time searching for something or someone to pull them out of their downward slump. Perhaps in seeking your purpose, you will find that you were created to pull someone out of a bad or negative spot in life. Those dreary and challenging seasons you've endured provided you with the energy and strength you need to move towards your purpose of positive intervention in someone else's life. You will be amazed to find out that life is filled with so many seasons, that you have a purpose for each one. Your perspectives will change with each season and the manner in which you respond will change also. As a juggler the realm of understanding becomes much clearer as the pins develop. Your purpose is not to quit, never give up but always push through and persevere. Your purpose aligns you with everything you need to successfully meet the demands of juggling every pin you have in your hand. Once you are clear on your purpose and realize that there is more than just one, it is then that you will be bold enough to fill each hand with pins and dare to make the juggle the challenge of your lifetime.

Rising to the Challenge (of the Demands)

For most women, rising to the demands of their purpose in life can seem a bit illusive. However, finding your purpose in life can be easier than it seems. It begins with the ability to identify the purpose in your life and use it to successfully answer to those demands. Tap into your talents, your life inspired gifts and use those to elevate the power of your strength in life. Juggle to your strengths. You already know that life can be difficult when you have only a few things going on but it really becomes challenging when you make the decision to juggle multiple pins. You've got this and you know what must be done. It is up to you to rise to the challenge of each demand you face. Many times you will find that much of the pressure you're feeling is a result of your consistent worry. Don't worry about what won't get done but instead, concentrate on those aspects that you can comfortably accommodate. A beneficial approach is to function on various platforms in an effort to discover what really makes you happy. This permits you to discover the areas in which you are most effective and most at peace while performing.

How often do you hear someone say, "I'm waiting on God to send me a blessing" or "I'm waiting on a sign before I..."? These are very common statements but are also common mishaps that lead to nowhere. Of course you should rely on your faith or whatever your belief may be to provide you guidance. However, don't waste time waiting but instead, save time by rising to the challenge. Make up your mind to be assertive in your passion to push through to your purpose. This means that you no longer sit around and wait to be asked to participate on a committee or perform during an event. It is now your purpose to place yourself in those places that you wish to exist. Your greatness is in your very own hands and they happen to be disguised as pins. Every task you take on, each obstacle you overcome and every challenge you face easily becomes the foundation of your purpose. Your responsibility is to yourself because you have now become your biggest critic. It is not a mental game but instead a personal agenda that must be satisfied in order for you to accept each challenge that comes your way.

Tell yourself again that you've got this, pick up your pins and sprint right along into the demands of your life. There is no way to ignore the fact that life can be demanding but what you can do is rise to the challenge and be more demanding of yourself. It is often seen that when you expect more, you give more. The pressure brought on by others will seem excessively minimal because you've already exceeded their expectations.

Listening to a radio show this morning and a listener wrote in with a personal issue. The objective of her letter was to find out if her standards were too high with the expectations she'd set for her life. The response given by the host was definitely aligned with my inner thoughts. He said, "never allow anyone to tell you that your standards are too high" and that is what you need to remember. Your standards must match your expectations and in some cases, exceed your expectations. How can you possibly expect to deliver greatness if you settle for minimal and set average standards? It is then that you begin to wonder why you are only getting the bare minimal from your efforts. Your juggling experience is everything but minimal and high standards are the building blocks of the approach that overcomes challenging demands. Let's take a look at how you can rise to the challenge in some cases. Take for instance deadlines, these are death traps that leave you stressing to catch up. This is not to say that you should not adhere to them but adjusting them will usually put you ahead of the game. If you know that the final draft is due by the end of the month, set your own personal deadline for the middle of the month and you will be ahead and never behind. This is all a part of your strategy to perfect the juggling of your pins. It is completely up to you to view the demands you encounter as opportunities. Move forward, ahead of those demands, in a place that allows you to juggle at your very own pace to develop achievement, reassurance and satisfaction.

Do you feel that your challenges are greater than those experienced by others? In some cases, they may be but keep in mind, you only know the burden that you feel by the challenges that are presented in your life. You have no real way of understanding the burden that is felt by others because it is not your load to carry. It is your responsibility to focus only on the weight brought on by your pins if you want to juggle them effectively. Creating a balance in life is the epitome of greatness in the success of juggling. Challenges will come and go in life and it is with each one that you strive to become a better person and a more effective juggler. As you set out to accommodate whatever the season may be in your life, you effectively do so by pushing through to your purpose and rising to the demands of every challenge. These factors place you in a position to manage and achieve each task that you have taken on in life.

You do know that pins come in all sizes and a few different shapes as well, correct? This works to your advantage in that choosing to pick up pins that vary in shape in size can make juggling much easier. Never back down from a challenge and always rise to the demands of whatever that challenge may be.

You are the controlling factor of every outcome because your determination pushes you through to your success.

Overdrive should be your gear of choice. This is the gear in which you are most effective and definitely most ambitious. Your determination to never give up is what will get you through each task, through each day and on to each new pin. Make a habit of pushing yourself for more and always expecting more than the norm. You must be willing to go the extra mile even when the GPS says that you have reached your destination, especially if the destination doesn't leave you feeling fulfilled. The faint at heart has no place in the world of juggling because it can and sometimes will, take your breath away.

Imagine being in a field of butterflies on a bright day, filled with sunshine. The clouds are a pretty blue and the ambiance is mesmerizing. You are almost lost in the moment when out of nowhere, swoops in a giant hawk that almost throws you off balance and causes you to forget about the beautiful moment you are enjoying. It is at that moment that you must decide to stand your ground and press forward or fall down and allow the hawk to overtake the magic of the moment you envisioned. You choose the latter because it is your season to push forward and existing in overdrive allows you to do so without second guessing yourself.

In acknowledging your season, you must also render respect to your circumstances. Are you a spouse, mother or in a relationship that requires a commitment of any kind from you? Do you value these relationships and view them as a vital part of your existence? If yes, it is crucial that you nourish them as well. They must be given the quality of attention that you desire from those who have committed to you. Most importantly, if you find that your relationship is suffering because you have too many pins in hand, it is time to reevaluate your juggling act. Never allow a relationship to demise because you were busy juggling other things of importance. Being an efficient juggler also means that you recognize those things in life that matter and care enough to balance them right along with your juggling act. Your spouse should not have to take on the full load of caring for the children in order for you to manage that pin you picked up. Your children shouldn't have to fend for themselves because you were too occupied with a pin that you forgot to buy groceries for dinner. If these things start to happen, don't just drop a pin, throw it out! No pin is worth your relationships and where you start is not nearly as important as where you finish. In most cases, your relationships existed long before you picked up the pins and you want them to be around even when you put these pins down. Juggling a hand full of pins is possible but only to be commended when you do so while juggling the joys of life as well.

Do you like coffee, or perhaps you prefer tea? Maybe your drink of choice is water or something fruity. Regardless of your preference, you are likely inclined to try something different from time to time. Maybe your choice is coffee everyday, you might require your coffee everyday, but the idea of drinking the new healthy green teas is calling for you to try something new in the morning. It opens you up to a variety of opportunities that you possibly would have never considered. This is the concept that you should incorporate into the balance of your relationships and juggling acts. Switch things up a bit and include your relationships in some of the tasks you've take on. This is only acceptable if it doesn't take away from the quality of time or nourishment of the relationship. Much of the strength and determination that you have when juggling, exists because of the love and joy you have gained from your relationships. It is because of these that you understand the feeling of greatness and accomplishment. Many times the people that you love most give you the inspiration you need to push through to your success and enjoy each season of your life. Don't allow them to suffer because you have elected to juggle more than you can balance. If you find that you are doing too much, drop a pin or two and pick it up later!

As you come into your season in life here are a few thoughts to ponder:

Your season in life will change and you have no control over it

- It is possible to have more than one purpose in life
- Juggling will be demanding and if it's not, you're not doing something right
- Challenges will come and with each one, you must rise to the occasion
- Shift your determination to overdrive and keep it there, it's the only gear that helps you to reach your destination

By applying these points to your life, you will find it easier to accept whatever comes and handle it appropriately. You have a lifetime to juggle the pins you encounter and you shouldn't expect it to be a dash to success. Patience is the platform on which you will erect a lifetime of pins to juggle and if your perseverance is strong enough, your patience will always prevail. Enjoy your seasons as they come and most importantly, embrace the change and remain steadfast in accepting what each has to offer.

"There can be no great accomplishments without risk" – Neil Armstrong. Each risk that you take is the turning point for your evolution of change and the strength of the direction in which your success is headed. You can choose to juggle the little things, the big things or mix them all up but what you can't do is give up because it is your season to push forward to your greatness!

CHAPTER 4

DO ALL PINS WEIGH THE SAME?

"You have within you the strength, the patience, and the passion to reach for the stars and change the world" – Harriett Tubman.

This is the phrase that you will need to repeat to yourself along your juggling journey because all pins don't weigh the same. This is a large part of what makes juggling so exciting, invigorating and rewarding. Discover the true meaning of happiness in life once you understand the difference in the weight of a pin and the burden of a pin. They both have the potential to inflict a challenge but distinguishing the two determines your ability to rise to the challenge. If you balance weight properly, you can and will reach for the stars but carrying a burden will weigh you down and prevent you from ever seeing the sky in which the stars live.

Are you prepared to pick up the pins in your life? What permits women to be most effective in their life is the determination to identify and transition the challenges they face. There are various approaches to be taken in an effort to transform the inner person. This is accomplished by identifying and dealing with the fears and challenges that occur in life. As a woman, remind yourself that the biggest and most beneficial change starts on the inside. You can develop the balance and strength needed as you work towards positive accomplishments in the world with each pin you pick up. Every challenge or tasks that you desire to balance is completely within your reach but you must make the decision to pick it up. Most likely, you're not afraid of the weight but fearful of how well it will balance with other tasks you have in your juggling cycle. This is why you learned to strategize and organize. You have a lifetime to juggle and it is absolutely essential that you always remember what you learned in the very beginning. It is the basics that built your foundation and your foundation will provide all of the support you need, no matter how much weight you add to it.

Most women have one of more pins or challenges that consistently appear throughout life. These challenges are typically grounded in the fears that accompany each pin as it is picked up. With the proper perspective, you can manage each challenge regardless of its size, because as you may have guessed by now, not all pins are equal in weight. Various pins will present different opportunities, obstacles and benefits in life. As a juggler, once you begin to view your pins as an opportunity, you have a greater chance of transitioning your obstacles into learning tools, which are the key to a better life.

Your pins are different sizes and some are even different shapes, but the manner in which you juggle them makes all of the difference in the world. The approach most women take when juggling their pins often originate from the things learned as a child. They can be a result of things they were told as a child. Negative or deterring responses from parents, teachers and other people of significance in life are primary scenarios. There are times when one or more negative experiences have an effect on the way women approach the pins they juggle as well.

If you're a parent, you are definitely familiar with the "it's not fair" battle cry. You have spent hours trying to ensure that you are equally dividing your time and attention between your children (and your spouse) so that they do not feel neglected.

One day I was riding in the car with my two precious children and before our departure, I had given them an even share of one of their favorite candies, Peanut M&M's. Everything was going well, we were having fun singing songs and just generally happy when all of a sudden my son bursts into hysterical tears.

Thinking something was horribly wrong, I immediately pulled the car over. I turned around to ask my beloved child what was wrong. He managed to say, between sobs "You gave Loren one more M&M than me!" (Yes my children had somehow managed to compare and contrast their M&M distribution in the midst of our family sing-along.)

I couldn't believe it! Here I thought he was going to say that he had a tummy ache or was going to throw up, or even that he needed to use the restroom. Instead he was seriously upset because he felt that I had shorted him a highly coveted Peanut M&M (which, to my children, are like gold and the magic cure for all that ails them).

If I had inadvertently miscounted the M&M's, thus resulting in uneven distribution, I was completely unaware. Of course, having been the mediator of many such arguments in the past, I certainly did not mean to give my eldest child one less M&M then his younger sibling. It was simply an oversight. But in the eyes of my child, it was a travesty. It meant that 1) I loved his sister more than him and 2) she got to eat one more M&M than he did, which was the real tragedy in this case.

Of course, I immediately composed myself and apologized profusely "Mommy is sooo sorry, baby, I didn't mean to do that." I felt horrible. In the grand scheme of things, in the eyes of an adult, it wasn't a big deal. But to my son with his red cheeks and tear-stained face, it was a major catastrophe, a betrayal of my love for him. He viewed it as nepotism on behalf of his sister and more important, missing out on his favorite candy. To him, that one Peanut M&M meant the world.

What I gathered from this traumatic situation (in the eyes of my child) is that sometimes, even though you have the best of intentions, you might make a simple mistake that could have a huge impact on the life of someone you love. Whether you were in a hurry, looking to take the quick and easy way out, or you simply made a careless mistake or an error in judgment, your actions have a direct effect on someone else.

Everyone has a different perception of the same reality. Someone else's expectations from the same situation may be totally different from yours. We need to be conscious of our actions at all time. And ready to react to any sudden "curve balls" that may come our way in the game of life.

Fast-forward a number of years. The same son, my dear Jared was the child that needed glasses to see, tutoring to keep up with his studies and little extra attention here and there.

However, he grew up to become an outstanding young man. He did not let his "limitations" hold him back. Rather, he faced his challenges head on and became an amazing young man of whom I will be eternally proud.

At times, it may seem as though some of our pins are just a bit heavier than the others. The red pin (say your eldest child) may prove to be a bit of a challenge for a season and then later on the blue pin (say your teenage daughter) may be the one that seems to be a bit more of a struggle. And even your favorite pin the green one (your husband) may seem to be a bit "heavy" at times. It's all about finding balance. You simply shift your weight and regain your composure. You take a deep breath and adjust to whatever life throws your way!

Examine or think back on your childhood or a negative experience. Is there a possibility that the reluctance you have in approaching certain challenges a result of said experience? You may be surprised to learn that there are many women who don't take chances today because they were often told as a child, that they couldn't do something or that a particular goal was out of their reach. It is necessary to disassociate those experiences from any juggling experience you may take on, because no two pins are the same and you are definitely not the same person you were as a child. The weight of your pins is largely manipulated by your mentality. This means that if you think a certain task or challenge is too much for you to handle, it will probably feel like a large burden on you. Don't underestimate your ability to juggle two or even three pins that seem to be heavier than the normal. If your mindset is strong and has the agility of a giant, you can manage those pins and more. Never allow the voices from your past that visit you from time to time to have a negative impact on your overdrive performance. From the very beginning, you set out to accomplish greatness, no matter what the weight and giving up is not an option.

Are you an overachiever? Does it feel like the more you have to do, the more you desire to do? This is a very strong, yet positive characteristic of a juggler. However, don't become the person that you try to avoid, the one who never feels that enough is enough. You could possibly be doing great with the pins that you juggle but in your eyes, it's still not enough. Reach for greater and always strive to achieve more but know your limits! Failure to recognize and honor your limits could eventually cause you to become burdened by one or more of your pins. This is another reason that it is important to map out your strategy for juggling and don't adhere from it at any time. If it seems your course of direction isn't leading you to the desired accomplishment, revisit the strategy for possible restructuring but never because you have the feeling that you're not doing enough. If you are on course and doing things as you originally planned, you are doing more than enough. Do not become an emotional juggler! The pin you picked up last month may weigh a ton and it is okay to not pick up another pin for a while. It doesn't mean you're failing but instead, you're winning at being the smart juggler that you are designed to be.

Examine your deepest fears, the things that prevent you from taking that leap or picking up a certain pin. This is the pin that weighs more than the others you pick up without fear. This is the pin that presents the greatest challenge or fear in your life. As a juggler, you will not feel accomplished until you pick up this pin and at least try to juggle it. Prior to picking it up, because you will pick it up, take stock of all other pins you currently have. Make certain that this pin fits comfortably with the others you are currently holding or juggling. It may be necessary to complete a juggle before approaching this pin and keep in mind, some pins are so heavy that they can be juggled alone. Come on, don't tell me you've never seen a juggler manage only one item at a time. It is possible and as a juggler of life's challenges, it is sometimes necessary. The pins that you juggle are all selected by choice but picking up one that brings out the fear and feeling of defeat in you will be a choice you will never regret. Although the start of your juggling journey may be structured with you juggling pins that are somewhat similar in size, it is not meant for you to spend the entire journey this way. There will be pins of all types and sizes that will attract your attention and some will even dare you to pick them up. As you become more seasoned in juggling, these become less of a challenge and more of a push for you to succeed.

The Push Pin

Have you given any thought to naming your pins? You know, add a little excitement to the journey along the way. It makes it much more interesting and possibly even gives you a bit more motivation as you push through each season. Have any ideas on what you will call them? One great idea would be to categorize them instead of naming each pin. For instance, those pins that you recognize as a challenge but not the biggest challenge could be the "push pin" or something similar. Pushpins will cause you to push yourself and get things done. This is a great way to describe those pins that you would likely procrastinate about juggling. Procrastination could easily cause you to drop the pin prematurely or remove it from the juggle cycle completely. This would mean that you gave up on a task or challenge and as a juggler, giving up is never an option. Every pushpin you hold is one that will elevate your strength in juggling. It is the one that actually helps to hold all others in place because it is not that difficult to juggle, if approached with a positive attitude and determination. Your pushpin can be any size you choose but make a point of picking up at least one during each juggle, they make great motivators for all other pins you hold in life.

Juggling pins is an art for most women and the approach is not the same for everyone. It does prove to be most beneficial to balance pins per their size but you must admit, it's much more fun to juggle them per your drive and determination. Once you have identified the pins that best fit the pushpin category, it helps to correctly class other challenges that you consider. Motivation is a major paintbrush in the art of juggling, and if you have just the proper mixture of motivation, determination and commitment, the juggling journey will be a sweet one to say the least. You will need to push some pins harder than others but that's to be expected because again, some are lighter in weight than others. The key is to keep pushing and if it seems the juggle is going just as you would like, it is then that you must push harder. Never become too comfortable in your juggling process because this is when most women lose their balance. You think you have everything under control and maybe even attempt to add another pin to the juggle but remember, proper proportioning of your pins makes a major difference in your performance.

One of the main goals in gathering your pins and starting to juggle is to feel empowered. As a woman, you are the epitome of power in any struggle you encounter, but especially as a juggler. It takes the strength of a giant because you will grow tired and sometimes feel hopeless, like you can't go on. This is normal and in fact, if you don't have these feelings, you may need to reassess your juggling act. Simplicity is a design, not a way of life. Your decision to add challenges to your life by juggling them at your own pace is one that will give you favor over the fear that has held you down for so very long. Understand the source of your strength, and deeply rooted in the creative design of every pin you approach. You are empowered and it is your juggling acts that remind you of this daily. Just as your pins are different, your days will be also. Some days you will feel that you have it all in control and nothing is out of your reach. Other days will feel like the end of the world and every pin you touch pushes you to the limit. This is when you must empower yourself with faith, determination, commitment and strength to push each pin forward and balance it until the task is accomplished.

Pins are also a source of your empowerment and you must view them as such. Don't allow your task or challenge to control how you approach the day but instead, remain in control of your feelings and drive during the juggle. Make every effort to categorize your pins and juggle them effectively each day. Doing so means that you are accomplishing goals on a consistent basis and picking up pins with equal consistency. Eventually, you will no longer consider overlooking a pin because you fear it will be too heavy, but will bulk up your strategy, bend at the knees and lift it to your hands for the juggle of a lifetime. The best feeling for a juggler is the one experienced during the juggler. There is nothing else on their mind but the successful tossing of what is in their hands. Focus is strong and everything around them is blocked out during the juggle because attention is on a successful completion of the cycle and nothing else. Pushpins are particularly great for any juggler because their presence causes the juggler to remain alert and focused as they balance. The chance for any pin to fall is greater when a pushpin is present. It may not be the heaviest, but is the easiest to put down without notice. Pick up a pushpin and remain focused until the task is complete. Every other pin in rotation will have a direct reaction to your focus and balance. You are the juggler and the amount of respect you demand from each pin is in your hands. Accountability is mainstream in every task you encounter and as you juggler, you must hold yourself accountable at all times.

The Straight Pin

Almost everyone you know has the potential to juggle a straight pin at some point in their life. But in juggling it, do you really understand the potential a straight pin has to strengthen your attitude, determination and presence in life? The straight pin is just that powerful land could be one of the least juggled pins there are. This category of pins includes those tasks or challenges that are presumably easy to juggle and therefore, mostly avoided. For example, you think because you have a degree in math, you could easily teach a group of elementary students. However, changes in teaching methods could present a certain level of difficulty if you attempt to teach students today and haven't had any continued training in math. Things have changed and common core mathematics is one pin you may want to study before picking up. This is another primary example of how all pins don't weigh the same.

Yes, you may be great at math but no, you can't teach a group of students how to excel in math, when you have no knowledge of new age math instruction. This is a perfect example of a straight pin. It seems easy, almost too easy, which causes you to not accept the task, but further examination proves that it's more of a challenge than you expected. Now you are inclined to pick up that straight pin that you almost overlooked. Once you have cited your intentions, develop an awareness of how and when you will approach this challenge. Each time you encounter a pin that seems to not be a challenge at all, take a closer look and confirm that your beliefs are correct. It could possibly be a straight pin that could be a great benefit to your attempts at balancing the challenges in life. Straight pins are not true to name, meaning they aren't always straight with no curves. In fact, expect a few curves with every straight pin you encounter. It is the curves that make it worthy of the juggle and your perception of its weight that determines the success of the outcome.

Another goal in juggling pins of different weights and styles is to create confidence in all that you do. Categorize your pins, but never yourself. Don't place limitations on the types of pins you pick up to juggle because as you move forward, you will find that no pin is too heavy for you. Confidence is key in every area of life but as a juggler, it is your defining characteristic. You must believe in yourself if you expect anyone else to do so. You must know going into each act that you have the strength and ability to juggle anything that you pick up and anything that is thrown at you as well. The confidence that you display, gives your pins permission to trust you. It may sound a bit out there but follow along to see the point. You never know who is watching you along your journey. Your children, family, colleagues and others will often pay close attention to the manner in which you tackle tasks with confidence and determination. Of course everyone that is watching, doesn't have the faith that you can or will do all you set out to accomplish. Allow that to serve as motivation to push you forward and continue to strategize with pins of all sizes. Your children, co-workers or others you lead must trust that you will make the best decisions for them, correct? Straight pins are almost the same because of your skill level in juggling them. Tasks that you may have undergone special training and know how to complete, will cause you to automatically assume they will be easy. These are straight pins and will always seem easy, which means you will hardly ever drop them or lose your balance while juggling. But wait, there is a chance that every straight pin isn't as it seems and once you approach it, the challenge could be greater than anticipated. This intensifies your level of commitment because you never imagined this to be the pin that presents such difficulty. When in fact, it's a simple reminder that not all pins are the same. Regardless of how much you thought you knew, as a juggler, you should always expect the unexpected, especially with the straight pins. As an empowered woman with confidence, you are prepared for any challenge that you encounter. Your strength and determination has manifested inside and it is now a normal part of your character. These are the traits that must be acquired and diligently embedded in the mind of a woman that juggles. She can't move forward, grow or excel without them. If she fails to develop these defining characteristics, every pin she touches will bring her pain.

Now that you know how to properly identify straight pins, it helps to know the best way to pick them up. Tasks or challenges that fall in this category don't have to be included in every juggle cycle. The truth is, you have more knowledge about the straight pins than any other pin you hold. You already have an edge because you have some underlying knowledge about the pin. Although you may not have a straight pin in every balancing act you perform, it helps to add them to the rotation at least every two to three cycles. They are great for the self-esteem and help to remind you as a juggler that there is always room for growth.

Yes, you learned how to bake the perfect pound cake when you spent all those Saturday nights in the kitchen with your mom.

But if you plan to prosper as a caterer, there are a few tricks that you should add of your very own.

This is just another prime example of how the straight pin seems like a challenge that you could easily accomplish because of your knowledge, but change in life makes it almost impossible to juggle it without at least a minimum level of difficulty. You have the capability to juggle any type of pin that you pick up. This is because of your ability to identify these pins prior to picking them up. Life is filled with challenges and because you have the proper traits, ambition and strategy, you can juggle these challenges without fear of failure. The absence of fear in juggling makes the experience much more enjoyable and the outcome one of excellence in every regard.

As you begin to assess the weight of each pin you juggle, you will find it easier to organize your approach. Be mindful of one important thing as you prepare to juggle. Pins may resemble in size, design and even color but could be entirely different in weight. This is why you must become accustomed to the idea of categorizing your pins, in an effort to prepare your mental and physical self for the lift. You know what each day holds when you take the time to prepare and strategize a solid approach to your juggling act. Never compromise the integrity of the tasks you have taken on by assuming you will be capable of judging a pin by its looks. The heaviest pins are usually the ones that appear light to the eyes. This is what causes a lot of women to lose their balance in juggling. The tendency to assume the pin will be easy and not properly prepare to lift it or juggle it, can cause you to lose balance at any time. Once you lose your footing, it may be more difficult to regain your balance and pick up the pins to start again. Although difficult does not mean impossible, it can mean lost time and in juggling the pins in your life, time is of the essence.

One of the most encouraging aspects of balancing multiple things (pins) in life is that it allows you to become better acquainted with yourself. You really get to know who you are deep down inside and most important, you work to become the best you possible. I'm sure you have heard of or known people who simply are not happy with themselves, their accomplishments or where they may be going. The decision to become a dedicated juggler helps to change all of these things for the better. The feeling of loving everything about you is one that many women long to experience. Making an honest effort to juggle pins of all sizes is the ambition that helps you to discover your inner courage. Ambitious, courageous and most of all, confident are only a few of the words that describes you and how you feel about yourself. These are feelings that may not have been a part of your life before you started this journey but they have been awakened, stirred and boldly displayed in all that you do now. This is the giant within you and it grows bigger with every pin.

As a juggler, you shouldn't expect all of your pins to weigh the same. This would make it a bit less challenging but not necessarily worth it. Here are a few points to ponder as you approach pins of various sizes.

- You define the strength within you
- The weight of your pins is determined by the strength of your drive

- Your confidence, ambition and success are the power points of your juggling
- A pin may be heavier or lighter in weight to you than it is someone else but your approach makes all the difference
- The value that pins place on your life is irreplaceable and will leave you with a feeling of accomplishment and joy

As people watch you juggle, some will suggest that a particular pin may be too heavy or not a good balance for that cycle of juggling. Remember that you are the person that committed to this and should never allow anyone to strategize or destruct the plan you have for your life. Balance is key and no amount of weight can throw you off if you remained focused and aware of the size of the pins that you add to your journey. You have prepared mentally, physically and emotionally for this balancing act. Don't add negativity to your healthy diet, it can destroy everything you've worked so hard to balance. Instead, bulk up those arms, clear all clutter from your mind and set your eyes on each and every pin as you toss it in the air. Now, stand firm and own any task you have your set on, regardless of how much it weighs.

CHAPTER 5

OOPS! I DROPPED ANOTHER ONE

Do you know someone who has so many things going on that you wonder how they possibly get it all done? Have you noticed that from time to time, much of what they start ends up taking forever to finish? It seems as if they start a project in January and it's almost a year before any results seem to surface, right?

Wait a minute. What was that? This sounds like you? Well, welcome to the journey of juggling, where pins will be picked up, dropped, picked up again and eventually, juggled to completion.

Feel better now? You should, because dropping pins is almost always guaranteed, but it's your reaction to the drop that classifies you as the "Juggler that Could."

When I started on my journey to begin my political career, I was ready to do all the necessary preparations and work to run for a political office. I had received my degree in Urban Development and my studies focused on planning cities and making them more livable, viable, and workable for successful living. I thought I was ready. I had never run for office, nor had I ever worked on a campaign. (I advise against that now) But I knew this was a juggling pin that I wanted to pick up. After obtaining the necessary signatures to secure my name on the ballot, the race had begun. Passing out literature outlining your position statement, attending neighborhood block club meetings, visiting and speaking at Rotary Meetings, Lions Club, Optimist Club, PTA/PTO's, kissing babies and shaking hands was all a part of the process. It was a grueling year, in addition to my other duties, responsibilities, and the other pins I was juggling. I ended up dropping this one, in my estimation by losing the race. I was unsuccessful in the race despite, in my humble estimations, of giving 110% percent. I dropped this pin a total of three times. I had 3 unsuccessful attempts to run for a political office. On the last attempt, I finally won the office of Southfield Michigan City Councilwoman and have successfully juggled that pin for a total of seventeen years.

The tasks you challenge are not designed to get you stuck, but to help you discover who you really are and what you want out of life. Some of the challenges that are being juggled may not even be ones that you picked up. You will find that some pins are thrown at you and may even feel that that they are destined to destroy you. More often than not, they are truly meant to push you to your greatness. These pins put you in the proper position to confront your fears by removing you from your level of comfort. Your strengths, weaknesses are manifested and in return, help you to grow into your true purpose in life.

Most women contemplate juggling for years before they take the steps to do so. The fact of the matter is, you don't truly live your life until you get your balance and stop hiding from the challenges that are meant to be a part of your journey. Here is a truth that many women don't want to or simply refuse to face during their course in life. No matter how fast you run away from challenges that are meant for you, life will find a way to trip you up and make you face these challenges. Life is about change and growth is a strong part of that change. In spite of all of your failures, challenges will help you to grow. Not all pins are designed to be difficult and some will even be very easy. Just as they don't all weigh the same, they won't all present the same obstacles. There will be ups and downs, trials and tests, lessons and limitations, but your strength and determination will help you to respond as you should. The adventure is like nothing you will ever experience and in your season, you will find that it was your destiny to take this journey.

Why exactly does life sometimes cause women to slip up while juggling? That's a fair question that deserves an honest answer, right? The question itself is one that is often asked but there really is no definitive answer. However, there are several reasons that could attribute to the occasional dropping of a pin while juggling. As mentioned, life is about change and growth. It is by facing and overcoming the challenges in life that women are afforded the benefit to overcome those challenges. This isn't punishment, but a lesson that all women benefit from at some point in life. The pins you take on require you to learn more about the areas of your life that need work. Once identified, you can work diligently to improve them and juggle a life you will enjoy. This aligns you to be prepared for those things that seem to come at you from out of nowhere.

As a woman who juggles, you will ask yourself what happens if you miss it? What if in all of your attempts to juggle, things don't go according to your plan? Considering the fact that you have invested a sizable amount of time, energy, focus and even money when juggling your pins, it can be deterring if things don't work out as planned. Yes. It seems like a big deal and in the grand scheme of things, it is a big deal. But you can't allow any minor or major setbacks to cause you to lose your balance. Don't ignore the signs however. Keep your eyes opened and focus on the objective of your desire. In essence, there are some pins that simply aren't meant to be a part of your juggling act. These are the ones that no matter how many times you pick them up and start again, they just won't work out. As a juggler, it will be possible for you to identify the pins that need to remain on the floor once they've been dropped. You don't want to waste time picking pins up over and over again, only to find yourself in the same situation. Your strategy, time and energy are too valuable to be wasted on pins that simply aren't for you. And only you can truly answer the question of which pins are for me.

As a juggler, you will find comfort knowing that none of life's challenges will last forever. This is a positive reminder whenever you find yourself struggling with the pins you have dropped or finding difficult to juggle. Don't allow the tests in life or these challenges to deter you from the goal you have set for yourself. Don't be discouraged because this is your journey and you are the navigator in charge. The end result is that you will be stronger than you have ever been and you will surely be more confident. Change the way you approach your pins and don't feel obligated to approach them all the same. You would hold a push pin completely different than you hold a straight pin and chances are, you would pick them up differently as well. There is no way to know which challenges will work in your favor and which ones will not. Knowing so may not be the best thing for you in the long run. It would remove the determination and the drive you have to always reach for the stars and be the best you can at all you do.

That's Not Your Pin

As you must know by now, life holds different meanings in each season. Equally so, each pin has its place and time in your life, but not all pins are yours to pick up. If every person were struggling to juggle the same pins in life, there would be no difference or significance among lives. You would actually become bored after a while if you watched others manage the same challenges that you have in life. There will be physical challenges, emotional challenges and let's not forget the spiritual challenges that occur. Don't make the mistake of thinking that you must pick up every pin you see. No. This is not what a juggler does in life. You must always carefully observe, consider and decide before you proceed to pick up. This may sound easy enough but you would be surprised to learn how many women are stuck in life because they are juggling, or attempting to juggle other pins that are not their own. Don't become this person. Learn what it takes to know which pins are for you and which ones you should avoid at all cost. There may not be a rule book but implementing the observe, consider and decide rule can and will save you from picking up the pins that may stick you where it hurts.

Observe the challenges that come before you in life. Make a choice to pay close attention to each of them and ask yourself a few questions in regards to each one. What will this challenge do for me and my growth in life? Am I equipped to handle the ups and downs that this challenge will bring? Am I accepting this challenge for myself or to appease others? Your answers are the cushions in which your pins will be inserted but keep in mind, your pillow isn't a full-body one. In fact, it's relatively small and equipped to hold only a few pins at a time. Careful observation prompts you to only have an eye for those pins that are meant for you, the ones that will give you the life that you deserve. You did know that challenges are life altering pins that women all over the world find to be a necessary motivator in the cycle of juggling? Could your world benefit from a few challenges that result in positive change? Take a look at the challenges around you, those you can't seem to get out of your head and you may just have observed your next pin.

Consider what your overall goals are in life as a juggler. This step causes you to revisit the point at which you first became a juggler. Consider everything, ranging from your options, the benefits, the pros and the cons of every pin you pick up. Once considered, take the time to ponder those thoughts and formulate sound choices on which pins appeal to you most. The time taken to give consideration to pins is a form of mental exercise. You are forced to think long and hard about what you are about to take on and how well you can manage it. This thought process is a necessary part of life, it's the warm-up for your balancing act. Failure to warm-up can easily cause you to catch intense cramps during the performance and drop every pin you've picked up. Here is another hint, every pin that looks appealing to the eye, won't be the right fit for your hand. In other words, it's perfectly okay to stare at the pin, it's part of the consideration process. But don't you dare pick that pin up. It's not yours and it's up to you to leave it where it is for its rightful owner. Don't' worry, you've got plenty of challenges to choose from and no time to deal with those that aren't your very own.

Now that you have closely observed and carefully considered, it's time for you to *decide!* Decide what course of action you will take, what strategy you will utilize and furthermore, how long before you balance the juggle. The decision process is without saying, the most intense but it is by far, the most important. It must be your decision to juggle the challenges that occur in your life. No one else has a say in what you do or how you do it but you have to make a choice. The decision is one that you will likely want to avoid but truly can't afford to do so. Women miss out on the most important days of their life because of failure or delay in making a choice. The eagerness that exist in learning a new dance, how to ride a bike or how to play your favorite sport, must be the same eagerness that burns within for juggling challenges in life. Women are cut from a different cloth and they have an inner strength and dedication to bring the impossible to pass. These are the core values that make women such passionate and successful jugglers of any tasks they encounter.

Picking up pins is not a hobby and should not be treated as such. It's an art that should be skillfully approached and meticulously orchestrated in order to enjoy a rewarding outcome. Challenges will come and they will go but what you must know is that some must be tossed aside. Walk away from the challenges that you know won't work well with your personality, drive and desire. If you are in doubt or just know that you can't handle a pin, leave it where it is. There are no judges in the balancing act of your life. Well, other than yourself and you should never set yourself up for failure. Realize that you can't pick up all the pins and then leave them for others to juggle if they choose to do so. Don't worry about them and once you've decided to move on, let them go and never look back.

Choosing the Right Pins

In the process of observing, considering and deciding which pins to pick up and which ones to leave down, one question is sure to arise. How do you know which challenges, passions or interests to pursue and what happens if not one of them appeals to you? A bigger question that is often asked is, what happens if you choose the wrong one. Have these thought and questions crossed your mind? Congratulations! This is further confirmation that you are meant to juggle, as these are questions that every juggler asks. The greatest fear is that you will take on the wrong challenge or maybe even nothing at all. Then you think that you are a complete failure because you chose the wrong path or did absolutely nothing. These are the negative thoughts, the clutter that you must clear out prior to starting your journey as a juggler. In the beginning, choosing the right pins will be challenging but as you grow in life, it will come easier. This isn't to say that you will never second guess if you are choosing correctly. But you will become more confident in the challenges you decide to approach. Until then, it is best that you learn to identify which pins are best for you and make a conscious effort to trust your decisions. You have to trust yourself in this process, or no one else will trust you either.

In trying to pick the pins that are best for you, don't waste too much time waiting for that "aha moment" that you often read or hear about. That moment almost never comes before you choose your challenges but most often shows up when least expected. The defining moment for most women will be when they observe and consider the pin that will create greatness for them. The one that will make them happy if it makes no one else in the world happy, you, the juggler will be happy. Your entire life transforms right before your eyes and it is the best feeling you've ever experienced. Again, this won't happen until you're well into the challenge and unfortunately, that won't help you during the decision process. Don't become discouraged. You will get your "aha moment", even if it comes once you've conquered a challenge. Whenever the moment hits you, it will awaken the sleeping giant within. It will lead you to become more curious about life and all of its challenges. You will find yourself exploring options that you never before considered, talking to people you know nothing about and eventually, choosing your pins based on knowledge acquired from these explorations and conversations. This is how you set the pace for selecting those pins that are best for you.

Many women often say that they know what needs to be done but still feel stuck in choosing the direction or deciding what to do next. This is quite common and there are a few things you can do to help elevate your level of comfort during your juggling journey.

- Succumb to your feelings – do more of what feels right to you. Listen to your "inner voice". It doesn't matter if others think or say it won't work. Tap in on how it makes you feel and capitalize on that feeling. Think about it, years ago you probably never considered changing the way you think to make life better for yourself. Today, you have made the choice to do just that. You may not understand the basics or the specifics but with a little exploration, that will change. No one has this part figured out at first. Stop beating yourself up. It is not required that you know it all from the start. To be honest, you will never really know it all. You may become a master juggler but the power to know it all is not a superpower that you will have. One thing you do know is that you are excited about the change that is about to occur in your life. You are prepared to do something important and rewarding, so you don't feel that you're wasting your life away.

- Select Pins that Overlap – this may sound frightening to think about it and perhaps a bit unrealistic at first but don't count it out just yet. It is okay to pick up more than one pin at a time. It's your choice and should be based on what you think you are capable of handling. In many cases, mixing pins is a creative and fun way to approach challenges in life. Some of the most creative and successful ideas in life are birthed from another idea. There will be some challenges you encounter that will be much easier to accomplish when approached in unison with others. Be creative! Mix those pins up.

- Find your Muse – this is a necessary part of the process for picking up the right pin. You would never attempt to bake a cake without having seen the recipe or building a house without a foundation. This is what your muse will do for you. She will be the model from which you form your strategy, your example. Identify a person or persons doing the things or overcoming the challenges you desire to achieve. Don't just close your eyes and blindly pick, but be selective in your choosing. Someone who has accomplished their goal or overcome a challenge would be ideal, especially if it is one similar to the one you are considering. Study their approach or how they accomplished what they did. Talk to her about the things she encountered, roadblocks or other obstacles that you should be aware or along your journey. Your goal is to gain understanding in order for you to originate a plan that will work for you. You will originate based on the knowledge gained from them, not duplicate.

• Build shelter for the storm – this is a challenge and obstacles, storms and hardships are to be expected. Don't run from the storms, they bring the compassion and appreciation for your challenges. The highs and lows will come at every point and every step will not be ordered. You will spend countless hours trying to get it right but that's okay too. You know that your greater is coming and you are working towards the dream of your lie. This alone makes the storm worth enduring.

The nature of building a new life for yourself is that you get the opportunity to learn new things, experience the positives and the negatives of them and endure the pain while doing so. This is what makes the difference. You will find that you have to rearrange certain aspects of your life while overcoming certain challenges. Prepare to get down and dirty in life if necessary but this only prepares you for the success you will welcome later. You may have to get a roommate, move back in with your parents or hire a babysitter or housekeeper for a while. The goal is to not lose focus on what you are working towards, the pin you have your eyes set on. The more you do, the more you will begin to enjoy the process. In everything you do, remember that if you never give up, it's impossible to fail because trying is not a characteristic of failure. In all that you wish you to do, try at least once.

It is possible to have your sights on several pins and not know which one is really for you. Take for instance attending college, many students enroll and start classes without declaring a major. They may not know what they want to obtain their degree in, but they know in order to graduate, they must start somewhere. This is a similar approach to choosing challenges with no true way of knowing what the outcome will be. You do however know that in order to accomplish the challenge at all, you must attempt it with a positive attitude. Another thing you've probably learned by now is that you must keep a positive attitude during this journey. It is the only way to defeat fear and the negatives associated with juggling. You have the right to pick up a pin and put it down if it isn't working. This may not be your pin to juggle and sometimes, you don't realize it until the juggling has started. Your attitude, determination and preparation make it easy to identify those pins that you should continue to juggle in life. One great thing is that pins will be plentiful, almost an overflow. There will be many for you to choose from and remember, they are not all yours. So don't feel bad about leaving some for others to juggle.

No pin is perfect, so choose at your own discretion. In life, there are no fair or unfair challenges. What's for you is for you and it's up to you how you approach it. Most of the pins are easier to pick up than they are to juggle. However, there will be times when you spend more time choosing a pin than you do juggling it. All of that fear and anxiety that led you to procrastinate for so very long, was for nothing. You can't judge a pin by its past. In other words, don't assume because everyone else says that a particular task is difficult that you should avoid trying it. They didn't have the tenacity or motivation that you do. Feelings and emotions are primary parts of juggling and once they get stirred up, the sky is the limit. Your outcome may or may not be what you anticipated but giving it your all guarantees that the outcome will be exactly what it should. You will notice the difference in how you felt when you first considered juggling and when you prepare to pick out the pins to juggle. At this point, you have made up in your mind that you will accomplish this task at all cost. Your passion and desire are burning deep inside and you can almost feel the greatness that is about to come.

Women who juggle and do it efficiently will be the first to tell you that they drop pins all the time. They find it a natural part of the cycle and in fact, expect to drop one or more on occasion. Guess what? The same will happen to you because you are human. I know, the whole superpower concept may have you thinking differently but some things can't be changed. Those pins are going to drop, you will have trouble choosing the ones that are best for you and occasionally, you will be forced to put down a pin because it wasn't yours in the first place.

Here are a few points to consider when breaking down the pin concept.

- Pins can be recycled. Therefore, you may opt to complete a challenge that someone else failed at before

- Your pins may have edges that stick you from time to time but don't be afraid to reposition yourself and start over

- Consider the benefits of any challenge you want to approach

- Observe the boundaries, pros and cons of all challenges you accept
- Decide what your strategy will be and how you can achieve the best outcome with any challenge

Your life has taken on an entirely new meaning at this point in life. Your views of obstacles and challenges have changed as you have made the decision to rise to the occasion and enjoy whatever season may come in your life. As a woman, you will experience mixed emotions and a rage of storms during your journey. Your natural abilities are all you need to make the most out of every attempt you make. Your choice of pins is strictly yours to carry and to later juggle but only choose those that compliment your personality, add humbleness to your character and give you a feeling of complete happiness in the end.

CHAPTER 6

KEEP YOUR EYES ON THE PINS

Your pins are probably all over the place by now. You may have several tasks in progress but because you are a juggler, this is expected. At this point in your journey, you are probably surrounded by pins and trying to determine how to keep your eyes on them all at once. Considering that we have minimal focus ability with the two eyes we have, it is impossible to watch them all at once. The phrase, "keep your eyes on the pins" doesn't suggest that you try to focus on each task all at once. Instead, it implies that you should focus on the goals you've set out to achieve, the pins you chose to juggle.

Too many times in life, it is easy to become consumed or side tracked by what others have going on. This is when most jugglers lose their balance because they lose focus on their own goals. This has a negative outcome for several reasons but most important, it could lead to disappointment.

Have you ever found yourself working on a project and someone you know is doing the exact same thing? It can be something as simple as designing a website, writing a book or entering the neighborhood cook off. It seems that no matter how dedicated and focused you are on your own project, you find yourself watching others to see how they are progressing.

There is no time to concentrate on what others are doing when you are truly dedicated to your own project. It can cause you to lose focus and even worse, compare your progress to theirs. The overall objective in every pin you juggle is to do your very best. You never want to sacrifice your potential by putting yourself down because someone else seems to be doing better than you in whatever the task may be. Another reason that is essentially important to keep your eyes on your own pins and don't worry about anyone else.

I'm going to share a story about my dog Jake and his innate ability to keep his eyes on the prize. Jake was a twelve-inch Shetland Sheepdog who had stolen my heart and has since left us to cross the "Rainbow Bridge" into "Doggie Heaven." But I will never forget the enormous impact he had on my life.

One day, early in the morning there were some city maintenance workers outside in our front yard. Jake had long since eaten his breakfast and finished his "morning stroll" outside. However, he knew precisely that he needed to go back outside so we could bark at the workers. He wasn't a biter, but he would bark at anyone who came too close to his turf. I recently said to him "No, Jake, you cannot go outside." But Jake was not taking "no" for answer. He was so focused on his goal of getting outside and defending his territory that I could almost see the wheels in his brain turning as he was exploring his options.

He immediately ran over to his food dish and took a few small bites of dog food (or quite possibly faked it, it happened so quickly). Then he scurried back over to me and looked at me with those big "puppy dog" eyes that had I had fallen for so many so many times on prior occasions.

Taken aback I said "Okay, boy, you win! You get to go outside. You did it, you outsmarted me and stayed focused to achieve your goal!"

You see, in our house, whenever Jake ate any of his food, he got to go outside, so he was simply using what he knew what worked to as the ends to his means. He kept his eyes on the prize and got exactly what he wanted. I didn't want to risk messing with all of his house training and years of success by refusing to reward his behavior. He used his training and potty habits to outsmart me.

So fortunately for Jake, he got to go outside and bark at the workers for a few minutes, much to their chagrin. He never once bared his teeth or tried to attack. He simply let them know "Hey, this is my turf, I'm in charge. If you wanna set foot in my yard, you'll have to get past me first!" He may have only been a barely-one foot tall, fluffy Sheltie, but in his eyes he was a menacing Rottweiler defending his castle.

Well, he met his goal! He came trotting back inside, tail wagging, a few minutes later, happy that he got to defend his turf. He knew that he had met his goal and he was quite proud of himself.

Dogs are much smarter than we give them credit for, they might not think on the same level as us, but they have their own way of rationalizing things. He knew that if he took even the smallest bite of food that I would let him go outside so he wouldn't have an accident in the house. He basically had me over a barrel. I knew he really didn't have to go outside and he knew I knew he didn't have to go outside, but based on weeks of training, and years of experience, he knew that his plan would work without a glitch. He not only got rewarded for doing the right thing, but he got to run outside and frolic and bark at some innocent city workers. He got to defend his turf and show them who was boss.

We can all take a lesson from my beloved pet. It's so easy to lose sight of things with the everyday stressors of live, but if we take a minute and just look at things simply, as in the eyes of a child, on in this case, the family pet, we can see things in a simpler way. There is always a way to reach our goals (as long as it is in fact, realistic) if we just keep our eyes on our goal.

So whenever you feel discouraged, just think of Jake, with his big, sad determined eyes...eyes that he refused to take off his goal no matter what life threw his way!

The motivation to work day in and day out can sometimes lose its sparks. This is especially true when working towards long term goals that will take months, sometimes years to achieve. The process can seem too tedious for the little progress that is being made and as a juggler, it is common to lose your mojo. It is now again that mental clarity becomes important, because the process of juggling some pins can be very painful. It may seem as if you are working towards something big but really don't see the end result manifesting anytime soon. This can be discouraging, but despite the outlook, you must think back to the reason you started and keep pushing. You will experience these moments as a juggler and sometimes they can be extremely overwhelming. It may be a good idea to take a break from juggling this pin. It doesn't mean to put it down and never pick it back up, but to lay it aside for a week or two. This allows you to return refreshed and rejuvenated with almost the same energy you had as you started the project.

Jugglers toss their pins differently and you must do what works for you. If your challenges or goals are of a long-term nature, expect to take a bit longer to successful achieve your goal. A long-term focus is required and bigger expectations often accompany these type pins. You are more than likely getting more done than the person who jumps from idea to idea and never getting anything done. Short-term goals are often easier to manage because they typically yield results quickly. Therefore, it doesn't take long to see your vision or objective come to pass. You may not have experienced the desire to give up but it may seem that you can't maintain focus and this can be deterring in balancing long-term goals.

Immediately you try and find ways to help you stay focused on your task in order for you to experience a successful outcome. Consistent focus ability is a primary skill for jugglers that desire to be successful. It is an imperative characteristic for those who wish to inspire others along their journey. A feeling of defeat or self-demise is common along any juggling journey. However, there are ways to maintain focus and your mental stability while juggling long-term goals in life. If the motivation and persistence is present, you can achieve it all because you believe in yourself. After all, isn't that why you became a juggler, because you can and no one else can tell you differently?

As a confident and goal oriented juggler, you will encounter negative feelings. These feelings are the fuel that keeps the fire to juggle burning deep within. In every pin that you pick up, remember that you must keep your eye on your pin. Imagine the difficulty of trying to juggle your own pin while watching someone else balance theirs. You set out with a primary goal in mind, to become a better you and make a difference in the world. You are doing just that and when you find yourself losing focus, address it. Don't brush it off as just a one-time thing. If it happened once, chances are it will happen again, and again, and again. Most jugglers are skilled at concentrating on what is in their hands and only that. You too must develop and perfect that skill. Nothing else matters when you are balancing the acts in your life. Your primary objective must be to get it right in your life and celebrate the joy that comes with this achievement.

Think of it this way, as a mother of a young child, you awake your school-aged child to prepare for school. Once they have arrived safely, you have done your part for the morning. Do you take the time to call to see if the little child that sits next to her arrived on time? Do you run next door to wake the neighbor for work? The answer to these questions is likely, NO. You focus on what is going on in your household, not the homes of others. This is the same watchful eye you must keep on your pins because you can't manage them possibly while watching others juggle.

20/20 Vision on Your Pins

Although it is understood that you should remain focused on your pins and your pins only, it can be challenging to do so at times. Take into consideration the fact that whatever long-term goals you are juggling, you are obviously passionate about them. Imagine a lifetime of juggling something you care nothing about, that's almost never going to happen. You invest endless time and energy into your goals and you will not allow a loss of focus to distract you and cause a less than successful outcome. This is why you must have 20/20 vision on your pins and always balance your values with your long-term goals and dreams in life.

Here is where you establish the necessary habits to maintain your focus as you juggle the pins throughout life.

Energy vs. Exhaustion

Where do you start? Keep in mind that you may want to consider juggling one long-term goal along with other short-term goals in an effort to create a manageable balance. Set specific challenges or goals for those areas that have validation in your life. Education, finances, family and work are primary areas to consider. Take the time to assess your goals and zone in on the ones that get you excited. Whatever you do, don't attempt to juggle a long-term goal that brings no excitement to your life. Doing so will get real boring, really quickly. Now, ask yourself do they excite you enough to work towards them for the next few months or years. Do you have the time and dedication it takes to bring these goals to completion? Most importantly, ask yourself is the goal or goals something that will benefit you in life or bring happiness to your life in some way.

Now erase from your mind any of the goals that don't get a resounding yes to any of the above questions. Revision is acceptable in some cases but make certain that the revised goals will be in sync with the "yes" answer to all of the questions asked before. These are the goals that will be consuming a large amount of your time, energy and thoughts. They will also take extreme amounts of patience because the positive results will take longer to see. As you add these pins to your juggling list, you must add equal amounts of passion and purpose because it will take each of these to accomplish whatever goal you set out to achieve. You've now separated the goals that are worth your energy from those that will simply leave you exhausted.

A Visual Perspective

Throughout life there are several self-help tips or motivation coaches that encourage you to do at least one thing, write down your dreams, desires, goals or plans. This is beneficial in many aspects of life including education, career, family, personal and you guessed it, in juggling. You must take a close look at your pins and always write down what you see and what you plan to do. This is an act of accountability as well. It's a good habit to not allow yourself to move on to another long-term goal before accomplishing the one you started first. You are your biggest critic, at least you should be and you must hold yourself accountable. Never count yourself out and it's easier to stay focused if it's in writing. Treat it as a binding contract between you and your happiness. This may seem a bit cheesy but you will find it to be the best part of your juggling strategy. Literally take a pen, sharpie, pencil, crayon, etc. and write your goals down.

Once you've written them down, put them where you can see them daily, several times a day if necessary. This presents a visual perspective of what you have set out to accomplish. Seeing is believing!

Here are a few great ideas to keep your pins visual.

- Write your goals or challenges on index cards and keep them in your purse, backpack, wallet or on the wall next to your desk at work.

- Technology gets us through the day and it can help to get you to your goals also. Set reminders on your phone, smartwatch and other devices that highlight your goals and remind yourself to work at it each day.

- Each step you take towards achieving your goal, reward yourself by taking a day off or enjoying your favorite hobby.

Self-Discipline

Life is a course that requires self-discipline in almost everything we do. As a juggler, this is absolutely imperative with every pin you pick up. There is no room for neglect as you work towards your long-term or short-term goals. You must understand that allowing yourself to fall short as you attempt to accomplish a task will deliver negative results in the end. We all have emotions and impulses, especially women but as you juggle various tasks in life, you must control these impulses and emotions. It's almost the main ingredient to any formula for achieving a long-term goal. No. it IS the main ingredient! Not everyone has the level of self-control they need when juggling but it can be developed. This is the characteristic that keeps you working towards the end result, persevering and focused. Self-discipline exists even when you aren't in the mood to work towards your goal. It pushes you to keep moving, reminds you to glance at the index cards that have your goals written down and will always make you stay accountable. Self-discipline is also an important element that keeps you efficient and faithful in your ability to accomplish what you started. It is the genuine belief in the fact that you can accomplish all goals, short and long. Sometimes you will need to give yourself a pep talk to keep or get you going. An internal foundation of control helps you to manifest the belief that you are responsible for your own success.

The Pin Cushion

As a juggler, there will come a time that you will begin to feel like a pin cushion. You are the cushion and all of your tasks are the pins- the straight pins that hurt! It is your responsibility to keep your pins properly spaced as you place them on the cushion. In other words, carefully manage your tasks by not overloading yourself and only take on what you can successfully manage. It is important to remember that you can always go back and add more as the pins are removed.

You are the juggler in this act and no one else has the right to push any pins into your cushion. You know this will happen and it probably already has. How easy was it for you to remove the pin that you didn't put in your cushion? Did it hurt as you snatched it out? Was the person shocked that you didn't allow them to add their pin to your cushion?

What?!! You still have it there? So, what you are saying is that you allowed someone else to add a pin to the stack you already juggle and you didn't do anything about it? This is not the road to success you have worked so diligently to pave. Up until this point you have worked incredibly hard to build up the courage to juggle, locate the pins that you find worthy of juggling, picked those pins up and started to move forward in your juggling journey.

And now, you allow someone, who has no interest in your success, to push their pin, big or small, into your cushion for you to juggle? Stop what you are doing and remove that pin right now. You know that it is impossible to successfully juggle your own pins while dealing with the pins of others. Everyone is not invested in your own success and those who add pins to your cycle are clearly invested in their own agenda. It is time that you take care of you in all that you do. The amount of time and energy it takes to remove a pin that isn't your own is minimal compared to the amount you are about to lose while attempting to juggle it. You must understand that juggling pins that don't belong to you will cause your own tasks to be at risk. There are only 24 hours in a day and no matter how you spin it, you can't get back time once it's wasted. At what point did you decide to allow someone else to ride your back while you juggle? It's not a comfortable position and almost impossible to balance. Take the necessary steps to remove the pins that aren't yours and begin by removing the negative people who don't respect your juggle and the things you are trying to accomplish in life.

Have you spent most of your life saying "Yes" to people and now find it a disadvantage as you attempt to juggle? As a juggler, you can't be a woman that always says yes. It will destroy you as you attempt to juggle pins in life. This is not to suggest that you close the door in everyone's face and never help. However, you must learn to put yourself first and only say yes when it is comfortable for you. A comfortable "yes" will not take you out of your zone or cause you to fall behind on your own goals in life. It will also not require that you put off something you are working on to help someone else accomplish their goals. Now, there are times when this will be what you choose to do but make it your choice and not the choice of someone else.

It is easy to tell others to learn to say no sometimes but not always so easy to take your own advice.

Here is a personal example of how it works to just say no, even to those you love.

My daughter recently got married. Following her engagement, she and I were off to find the perfect wedding dress. My husband and I being a little old fashion, expected and wanted to pay for the wedding dress. Well, along the way, my daughter applied for the television show, "Say Yes to the Dress", every bride watches this show I'm sure.

Meanwhile, we had given her a budget of the amount we were prepared to pay for the dress and were all in agreement. Well, my daughter was selected to appear on the television show and we were off to Atlanta, Georgia for taping. Upon arriving at Lori's Bridal, we again discussed and agreed on our budget.

Once we entered the store, the display and array of wedding dresses was fabulous. A few of these were in our price range. I say repeatedly, a few! Need I say more? Well, my daughter did not stay focused, she was overwhelmed.

I wanted to share this story for several reasons: (1) You must learn how and when to say no, even when it is extremely difficult; (2) You must learn how to say no when situations do not align with your vision 3) You should not put yourself in a situation that you know will leave your vulnerable 4) Don't allow the pressure others around you to go along with your when it's outside your limits.

The bottom line is this. I stuck to my budget and my daughter selected a dress that was slightly over and she paid the difference. It was a beautiful dress but there were also some lessons learned along the way.

Here are a few tips on removing pins that aren't your own from your pincushion.

- Develop a wall that doesn't allow others in unless you invite them. This means that you will remain in control of your time, resources and availability and sometimes you have to let people know that you don't have the time and won't be available to them for a while.

- Cover your pincushion. This simply means that you will develop somewhat of a tough skin. You won't be rude to people but they will know that you are not easily accessible and won't be manipulated into putting your own goals aside for theirs. You don't have to tell others what your goals or challenges you are working towards but make them aware that you have your plate filled with things that are important to you right now.

In order to successfully reach your goals, it is important to stay focused, driven and dedicated. Time management is an essential tool that allows you to successfully work towards your long and short-term goals. Develop the necessary habits to make achieving your goals easier. It is impossible to maintain a good balance while maintaining bad habits. Some of the things that you wasted time on before will need to take a backseat to your passion. Excessive television viewing, social media addictions and attachment to your mobile devices can be negative distractions. Once you have aligned your goals, it is up to you to stay focused in working towards them. No one else will see or appreciate the value in what you are juggling like you will. Becoming a juggler was a great decision because it allows you to live a fulfilled and happy life, but with some effort on your part. You will notice that as happiness is gained, a few acquaintances will drop off along the way, but that's okay, as long as you don't allow them to drop your pins.

The Boredom Culprit

You wake up to the sound of your alarm clock and immediately you're reminded of all the things you have to do today. On top of everything else, there's the laundry, lunch for the kids, mail run and oh yeah…you can't forget that big goal you're working towards. The thing is, you haven't forgotten it but wish you could because the truth of the matter is, and you're growing relatively bored with the process. This can't be good but guess what, it happens to the best of jugglers. It's known as the boredom culprit. You know what has to be done and have spent the past few months doing this very thing but when can you take a break or maybe switch things up a bit is what you may be wondering. One thing for sure, you don't want to give up but simply wish it wasn't so blah! Change is good and as the juggler, you have the power to change things up a bit.

Boredom sets in when one least expects it and it always seems to arrive at the most inopportune times. For instance, you begin a project, excitedly work on it for a while, eventually lose your focus and start working on something else. It becomes a cycle until you realize that you are juggling several pins with no real end in sight. You aren't making any progress and for a juggler, this doesn't make the task any easier.

Don't worry, it happens to the best of jugglers and is completely normal.

As I discuss this, I'm quickly reminded of a friend who was sharing with me her story. One day that she was at the club practicing on her tennis game. There was this tennis pro coach visiting who had influenced thousands of tennis players during his time, including a few notable favorites.

She had just wrapped up her session when she approached the coach and asked, "What's the difference between the top athletes and us normal people. What do they do that most of us don't?"

She smiled and pondered for a moment before saying a few expected things. Luck. Skill. Talent. Genetics.

But what she said next caught her by surprise.

She said that it eventually boils down to who is prepared and has the mental psyche to handle the boredom of consistency. The boredom associated with showing up to the tennis courts daily and swinging time after time until you're sore and can hardly move your arms.

I was surprised but deep down, I understood what she meant. It's about work ethics and the ability to remain focused on your pins.

Often peoples speak of being motivated or pumped to work towards a certain goal. It is at that very moment that they exude the passion and determination to accomplish this one thing. As a result, it takes passion for the pin. You must be passionate about every pin you pick up.

Because of this, I believe that people become discouraged when they lose focus or lack the motivation because in their minds, those people who have succeeded have some sort of endless passion and drive that they can't seem to hold on to. However, the tennis coach described it to be the exact opposite.

Instead, she indicated that people who have found success in what they do encounter the same boredom, lack of drive and determination that everyone else feels. They don't have a special potion or solution that causes them to wake up every day feeling inspired to do what they do. The difference is that those who stay on track and stick to their goals don't allow their emotions to overrule their actions. People at the top of their game, those destined to achieve their goals, will find a way to show up, overcome the boredom, and to embrace the daily steps required to successfully accomplish their goals.

What separates the successful jugglers from those that fail? It's their ability to put forth the effort and do the work when it doesn't come easy and the will to never give up. This is the difference between winning and losing at whatever goal you set out to accomplish. Because you are in control of the outcome of the pins you juggle, you must also be in control of the feelings and emotions you have as you juggle from day to day. Learn to answer to the cries of your emotions and not ignore them. This allows you to move away from those emotions that make you feel less than capable of accomplishing your dreams.

Here are a few things to ponder as motivation to keep your eyes on your pins.

- Work, even when it's hard to keep going
- Learn to appreciate the process, not the outcome
- Remain consistent in working toward the goals you have written down
- Don't become distracted by others around you, keep your circle small and your wall tall

Jugglers must understand that throughout the process, it's common to lose sight or focus of the pins being juggled. It is okay when this happens but you must immediately zoom back in on what's important to you. Disregard any negativity or interferences from those things or people in life who are not a part of your process and focusing on your own pins will be much easier. Every pin you pick up should be carefully observed before doing so. You want to be careful and not stick yourself in the process of picking it up or juggling it.

Find your happy space as you juggle and always look forward to moving one step closer to completing your goal. Every contribution you make towards achieving the goal you set is one that will help to clear the path for a well-balanced journey. Just as you view other things in life with caution, your pins should be viewed the same. Your goal is to pick up only those pins that are meant for you and to develop ways, places and times to juggle to prevent boredom from taking over. The most important aspect of all, balance yourself with determination, eagerness and a clear picture of what you plan to achieve with the pin you have your eyes on.

Chapter 7

Staying in Rhythm

Juggling your pins is strictly about the rhythm right? While it may not be about rhythm in its entirety, it is a major part of the entire juggling act. The ability to stay in rhythm helps you to feel more in sync, more accomplished and more in tuned with what's going on in your life. A patterned rhythm will help you to remain focused on those things that are important to you and the things you are trying to achieve.

The process that leads up to becoming a successful juggler can be overwhelming but it is worth every unsettled feeling. At this point, you are juggling, hardly ever dropping a pin and when you do, you bend over to pick it up and never lose your balance. This is now the new you and every part of you is working towards building something great. The pins are aligned, they're in position to go up when you want and come down as needed but best of all, you're doing it with a rhythm that you established. This rhythm is what works for you and no one else. Even when it seems that you're completely off beat to everyone else, it won't matter because only you know what it will take to stay balanced, juggle those pins and meet your goal. You are now dancing to your very own beat and it's the sweetest tune you've ever heard.

Establishing and maintaining a rhythm doesn't mean that you will never lose your balance or get off beat, because you will. It's natural to take a step to the left, when you should be going to the right. Although natural, it is only acceptable if you reclaim your position and get back in rhythm as soon as possible. If you allow yourself to stay out of rhythm too long, you will find it almost impossible to get back in stride. Once you have danced to your own tune for so long, it is almost impossible to dance to the tune of anyone else. The music is loud, the melody is in your heart and the passion cues every step you take. This is the rhythm that propels you towards successful completion of your goal and it is the only rhythm you should acknowledge.

Rhythm Breakers

Jugglers must be keen at identifying rhythm breakers, the things that interfere with their rhythm. In order to get rid of or avoid them, it helps to know what they are. You have taken the necessary steps to achieve your goals by changing your behavior and creating a better you. This all played a major role in establishing your rhythm. The moment you started to eat, breathe and sleep consistency is the moment your beat gained its rhythm.

Here are a few places to start in order to rid the dance floor of anything that causes you to get out of rhythm and lose your balance.

Perfectionism- Don't become over taken by the idea that everything you do is perfect. You know you make mistakes and perfection should not be your ultimate goal. Failure to appreciate every step of your process as you work towards your goal can cause you to lose your rhythm. To avoid this from taking place, pay close attention to the little things you do that put you one step closer to achieving your big goal. Without the little steps, you will never reach your destination. Be consistently appreciative of the talents and skills that you have which allow you to work towards your goals and don't allow what others have accomplished to cause you to cast a negative shadow on your efforts. Don't strive to be perfect but work endlessly to be pleased with all that you do.

Failure – I wish I could help you to erase this word, this thought from your vocabulary. Failure is not a part of your life or anything you set out to do. The only person who fails is the one who never tries and if you have made it this far, it's clear that you have tried. Too many people see obstacles or roadblocks as failure, when they are merely nothing more than stepping-stones. These obstacles can be a blessing in disguise that keeps you from something that wasn't meant for you or helps to design a different path to get you to it. Your determination and drive are the giants that defeat any thoughts of failure because you will come out stronger in the end than you were at the very beginning. So, instead of thinking of every delay as denial, view it as an opportunity to rethink, reconstruct or reevaluate your initial approach because failure doesn't exist among the pins.

Finish Line – Everyone starts a goal with the end result in mind but focusing on the outcome will cause a juggler to lose her rhythm every time. This reverts back to the advice that suggests you should enjoy the process and dwell only on the steps they are being taken. You don't spend the months leading up to your birthday, celebrating your birthday do you? Well, that may depend on how much you look forward to growing old in life but most people take them as they come. You must treat the concerns surrounding your goals the same way. You know that the end result will be great and it will arrive in due time but don't spend time worrying about how long it's going to take. Doing so robs you of the opportunity to enjoy the journey that helps you to reach the finish line. Don't lose your rhythm by stretching your arms to touch the finish line that you can't even see yet.

Big Steps –In learning to dance, you should not be taking big steps and you shouldn't be doing so in juggling either. This is the perfect way to lose your rhythm. You may be eager to achieve your goal. We'll call it excited but don't take giant steps that will likely throw you off during the process. It is best to take small steps to maintain a cordial rhythm. This is what most successful jugglers find to help them with balancing several pins. Consider this, you took your time to select the pins you juggled. You carefully observed them, selected the ones that work best for you and made the decision to juggle. Don't ruin the entire process by taking giant steps that could cause you to miss the best parts of your juggle dance.

The Unexpected

Every juggler will tell you that assuming the role of a lifetime juggler is a wonderful idea but it does come with it downsides.

One of the most talked about downside of juggling to achieve goals in life is life itself. Yes. Life is what you have each day that allows you to wake up and juggle those pins you've chosen. Life is also what happens when you least expect it and could cause you to put down every pin you've ever picked up. Those unexpected things in life that catch you off guard and completely throw you off rhythm. Oh yes! They will happen but it's how you respond that's make the difference.

Let's face it, there will be some things that happen in your life that will decrease the possibility of achieving a certain goal or reaching specific accomplishments in life. The first rule is to get over it! This may seem harsh but it's necessary. Don't waste time sulking about things that you have no control over or can't change.

Your goal of starting your very first backyard garden and bringing vegetables to harvest is an extraordinarily realistic one. But you have no control over the extremely hot weather that would kill your plants or the drought that starved the plants and prevented them from growing, or even the deer that ate them! You can't control the unfortunate fact that the one class you had to take in order to graduate next semester is not offered and you will be forced to wait longer for your highly anticipated graduation.

Although these are extremely dire circumstances that have the potential to alter your plans, it doesn't mean that your plans can't be accomplished. It simply means that you will be required to restructure your strategy to achieve this goal later. Life happens and sometimes, it has no respect for the rhythm you've established. If you are determined to accomplish what you set out to do, you will not allow circumstances that are beyond your control to mask your motivation. Pick up your pins and place them on the shelf until it's reasonably safe to resume your progress. You can continue to mentally and emotionally work towards your goal, even when you can't make the physical effort to do so. Your choice to accomplish greatness in life didn't have a preset rhythm but it's what you established along the way. You control the ability to start and pause your rhythm at any time but the important thing is to never LOSE it!

It is often that jugglers disturb their own rhythm as well. This is easily done and often overlooked. You want to be sure to not get in your own way or step on your own toes by coming up with excuses along the way. Excuses are big rhythm breakers and will creep up on you at a moment's notice. It is easy to make them without realizing you've done so and before you known it, your rhythm is completely off and you can't tell if you're juggling pins or throwing fire. Jugglers don't necessarily mean to make excuses but again, they are a part of the unexpected.

Are you a juggler that allows excuses to cause unexpected delays in your process? You may be doing so without awareness. Here are a few of the most common excuses that throw you off of your rhythm.

You're not ready! You want to do something but maybe you're not ready to do it. Ask yourself, "why not" and see what answer you get. Are you not ready to experience the success or not ready to put in the work? Either way, you're delaying your own progress.

Timing isn't right! You are determined to get it done but just not right now. When will the time be right? You have the skill, the mindset and the tools to get it done but you keep waiting for the right time. This is the excuse that forces you to revisit your ability to recognize your season in life. The only time you have is right now because tomorrow isn't promised.

You're not good enough! This is one thing and only one thing, an EXCUSE! As a juggler, you have the tenacity and energy to learn anything you set your mind to. Devise a plan to reach your goal, decide what it takes to do so and set out on your mission. The mistakes that occur, the depression that sets in and any other deterring emotions are only esteem builders to help you see that you are more than enough!

People will criticize you! You are exactly right on this one but it's just an excuse if you allow it to prevent you from moving forward towards your goal. This is a rhythm breaker that you allow to enter your otherwise melodious mental space. People will criticize what they don't do. It's human nature but guess what, deciding not to attempt or finish a goal isn't going to stop people from being critical in your life. Look over the negativity and hop right along to the next step towards achieving your goal.

Everyone else fails at it! This is the oldest and lamest excuse on the dance floor. You could be the very one to master it and remember, if they tried it, they didn't fail at it. You only fail if you fail to try. Your determination and motivation must be consistently aligned with your rhythm in order to maintain a healthy pace while juggling everything in life. You won't know who failed if you keep your eyes on your own pins and not focus on those of others.

Music to Your Ears

Have you ever listened to a song and long after it has ended, you still hear the rhythm in your head? This happens to a lot of people and what's most frustrating is when you know the words or the rhythm to a song but for the life of you, can't recall the name. This is the impact that rhythm has on the life and success of a juggler. The pins become music to your ears and before long, it's all you really hear. Your passion, energy, drive, motivation and eagerness to reach your goals are all set to a systematic rhythm that you developed. The beauty of it all is that you control the play speed, the volume and the times at which it is played.

Juggling pins in life is a process for everyone who does it but you have not accomplished anything until you realize that not everyone will juggle to the same beat. This is why you must control your own pins and never attempt to control or juggler the pins of others. The objective is to continuously play your favorite melody as you juggle. It is possibly a tune that no one else has ever heard, but that's okay because you're the only one dancing to the beat. One thing that you must realize is that you don't have to juggle at any set pace. Yes, setting goals with end times is a good idea but don't pressure yourself. There will be times when you have to stop working towards a goal to deal with some unexpected thing. Don't allow a change of schedule to cause you to have a change in heart about accomplishing something you've dreamed of for a very long time.

Each goal that you accomplish, no matter how big or small, will ring a resounding melody in your ear. It is a feeling of accomplishment that becomes an addiction for a juggler. There are so many addictions one could have in life but one of accomplishment is one for which you need no rehab. You don't want to stop accomplishing things but you become more determined to get things done. It becomes a must that you set goals and once one pin drops, you rush to pick up another.

Jugglers do this because they never want to lose their rhythm and never want to hear the music stop. You are dancing to your own beat and for the first time in your life, you don't want the music to stop. This is what accomplishment feels like.

All of the excitement and eagerness that comes with achieving your goals can lead to many changes. Changes in your lifestyle, changes in your perspective in life and changes in the way you cope with these changes as well. As you adjust to life as a juggler, it is essential that you remain humble. Don't allow your success or drive to push you off the deep in. This is the quickest route to demise than any other. This is no suggestion that you shouldn't be proud of your accomplishments, because you should. But don't allow the things you accomplish to change the person you are on the inside. You were pleased with yourself before you became a juggler but now you are in a state of happiness and you want to live there for the rest of your life. Losing your humble nature can make it difficult to continue on a juggler because you begin to assume that you can do it all. You start to believe that you are owed things of which you are not. You can quickly and easily lose your grounding and this will surely kill the rhythm for every tune you attempt to play as you go forward. Enjoy the process. Acknowledge the progress. Celebrate the end result. Repeat!

A Song that Never Ends

You begin collecting your pins but you truly never collect them all. Juggling is something that you will do for a lifetime and with the end of each cycle, you look forward to the next. The song begins, the lyrics sound great and eventually, you've developed your very own rhythm. Take a moment to celebrate every goal achieved and remember to not take too much time off between pins. In the essence of it all, juggling is just the process of adding more spark and excitement to your life. It's your way of ensuring that things will never be boring and there is always something to do in life. It paves the way for you to work towards something great, without ever feeling like the end is near. Celebrate the note in each tune and share your accomplishments with those who cheered you on along the way. Remember that pin you picked up when you first started juggling but put it down a while back? Go ahead and pick it up again, you're just where you need to be in life to make it through that cycle this time. The truth is, you don't need the pins, but they need you because otherwise, they have no life.

In all of the pins that you have juggled, you had no idea that you were writing music did you? That's exactly what you've done. You have worked tirelessly to achieve some of the greatest moments of your life and there is much more in store. You found ways to make things work when it seemed impossible at first. You took your drive and determination and turned it into passion for greatness. Everything you did and everything you accomplished was a verse in this song of yours. Life has allowed you to put it to music and it sounds like nothing you've ever heard before, it's like sweet music that lives in your heart.

Women who juggle have a kind spirit but a roar of a lion. The kind spirit is needed because they must have passion that lives within them. The lion's roar is the intensity at which they approach everything they set out to do in life. Your roar becomes your signature and your kindness is the paper on which it is signed. Move forward without ever looking back because pins left behind are those not meant for you in the first place. Always set your sights on achieving greatness and you will never settle for less. Your ability to comfortably blend family, work, social living and other things with your pins is further proof that you have mastered the concept of juggling.

In every pin you pick up to juggle, you must remember why you started. This is key in making sure to juggle it till the end of its cycle. Knowledge of why you set out to do something is often the fuel you need to get it done. If it was important enough to write down and look at every day, it's important enough to do it without giving up. Keep in mind that although you are like a professional juggler in many ways, there is one way that you are completely different. The pins you are juggling are not for entertainment purposes. They are collected as an attempt to fulfill your life, not entertain others. This is why you must remain focused and never lose sight on why you are the juggling woman that you are. No matter where you are or where you go, your drive, determination and your rhythm stays with you. Because of this, it is easy to juggle to the beat of your own drum and always maintain the perfect balance.

Even after taking every necessary precaution, writing your goals down, looking at them every day and staying motivated, chances are, you will still find yourself uninspired from time to time. There will even be times that you forget all about one or more of the goals you set. This happens when you become comfortable in your routine and don't always utilize the visual aids that are suggested. It happens to the best of us and it will happen to you also.

So, what do jugglers do to remain inspired and not forget about the goals during their juggling journey? Although, you will be faced with the sad possibility that you won't complete every goal you have listed. This is not entirely bad because some of them you put down by choice, while others may have been dropped by chance. There is a simple strategy that could possibly help you to complete almost all of the goals you have. This strategy involves making every effort to keep your goals in your presence at all times. Again, keep your eyes on your pins! Naturally, you won't spend each hour of the day thinking of your goals but it is possible to keep them visible at all times. As they say, out of sight out of mind. By keeping your goals in sight, they will stay on your mind.

Read the goals that you took the time to write down and make a habit of doing so each day. Post them on the bathroom mirror to see while brushing your teeth or curling your hair. Stick copies on the sun visor in your car and read each time you enter or exit the vehicle. Visual aids are significant tools that assist in many areas of life. Just as you hear the rhythm of the pins you juggle, the visuals help you to see the rhythm as well. There is no timeline for accomplishing greatness. The fact is, you plan to spend the rest of your life making a positive impact on others and feeling better about yourself while doing so. You have finally realized that juggling has allowed you to face fears, overcome obstacles and create a new identify for your inner-self. The feeling you have once you wake up in the morning is unexplainable. Although your plate overflows, you don't mind sitting at the table because you know that there is no need to overindulge. The pins on your plate will be there until you take them off and won't be removed until then.

You are to be commended on your decision to become an efficient juggler. You have all of the tools in place to make this journey a successful one. The control that you have over your life at this very moment is magnificent and you really can't get enough. Everyday isn't as you would like but this causes you to do everything you can to make each day, one you will remember.

You are a juggler, but there will be times when even you need a little reminder. Here are a few points to ponder to keep you on track towards achieving your goals:

- The decision to juggle was your choice
- You must focus on those things that are important to you
- Pins are a part of your daily life. You can spend your life stepping on them or picking them up to juggle
- Your outcome is only as strong as your determination
- It is okay to start over if a pin drops or life knocks one out of your hand
- Juggling is not for the faint of heart but for a well-rounded, determined and motivated woman who has a passion to succeed in life

You have probably juggled a few different pins by now and feel that you are well on your way to becoming the queen of juggling. You are indeed a fierce weapon when working towards your goals. The key is to keep pressing, thinking and executing. Never give up! Always think outside the box and consider new ways to work towards your goal. Move forward, strategize and put those pins to work as you balance them from day to day. The process will at times seem too fast and you will sometimes lose your step. But the success will overshadow all negative and remind you that all along, you were in rhythm with the plan you designed for your happiness.